SEASHORES

A GUIDE TO ANIMALS
ALONG THE

by
HERBERT S. ZIM, Ph.D.
and
LESTER INGLE, Ph.D.

Illustrated by
DOROTHEA and SY BARLOWE

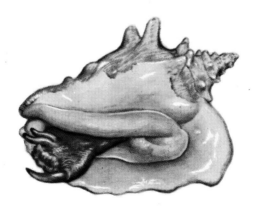

1991 Scholars Edition

GOLDEN PRESS • NEW YORK
Western Publishing Company, Inc.
Racine, Wisconsin

FOREWORD

Where land and ocean meet at the shore a mysterious world begins. Here the drama of the sea and its life comes to a focus. This book—a seashore primer—will help you understand and enjoy this unique zone.

Many persons helped to make our book possible. First to be thanked are the artists, Sy and Dorothea Barlowe, for their excellent work. Valued suggestions and criticisms came from several experts: E. J. Alexander, Frederick M. Bayer, William D. Clarke, John E. Fitch, Ira N. Gabrielson, Melinda M. Godfrey, Paul J. Godfrey, Howard R. Hill, Joan Lockhart, Alexander C. Martin, Harold A. Rehder, Paul C. Silva, and Alexander Sprunt IV. Donald F. Hoffmeister, Natalie and Milton Zim, Frank C. McKeever, Rosalie Weikert, Donald P. Rogers, and S. A. Farin helped with source material. The New York Botanical Garden, American Museum of Natural History, Smithsonian Institution, Philadelphia Academy of Natural Sciences, Los Angeles County Museum, and University of Illinois Natural History Museum also gave generous assistance.

H.S.Z.
L.I.

Revised Edition, 1989

HOW TO USE
THIS BOOK

The United States has about 88,600 miles of tidal shoreline, and nearly every mile is a place of potential interest. Everything on the shore is worth your attention, from the magnificent sweep of the sea and sky to the forms of life that dwell on the beach or are cast up there. Hunting for shells has

Rainbow Jelly—a Comb Jelly

long been a favorite pastime. This book will help in identification, but it is more than a guide to shells. It attempts, in a simple way, to give a picture of life at the shore, from soaring gulls to worms and clams.

You can use this book best if you begin before you go to the shore. Read these introductory pages. Thumb through the book to get acquainted with marine plant and animal life. Remember that shells and seaweeds cast up on the beach may look quite different when they are dead than when alive. Remember also that, yard for yard, some shore areas are much richer in life than any other areas. Don't expect to identify everything you find. Use the key on the next two pages as a starter. With its help, you can place most things within a major group. Then look further to see if your specimen or one like it is illustrated. Illustrations show only a few of the most common of thousands of species. Yours may be similar to, but not identical with, the one illustrated. Sizes given are average; allow for variation. For more detailed identification use scientific names (pp. 154-157), the books listed on p. 154, and museum study collections.

ALGAE — non-flowering and of varied form; seaweeds. **18-35**

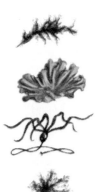

Blue-green Algae (1,500 species) — threadlike or branched filaments; some slimy. **20**

Green Algae (5,000 species) — some sheetlike; most are branched or unbranched threads. **21-24**

Brown Algae (1,000 species) — mainly large, cold-water plants; often with air bladders and "leaves." **25-30**

Red Algae (2,500 species) — smaller, more delicate than brown; live in deeper, usually warmer water. **31-35**

FLOWERING PLANTS — a great group (250,000 species), with roots, stems, leaves, flowers. Only common dune and shore species are included. **141-146**

SPONGES (3,000 species) — simple, many-celled animals with numerous pores; varying form and kinds of skeleton. **41-43**

CORALS and KIN (5,000 species) — soft, cuplike, with tentacles, stinging cells. Some have limy skeletons. **44-52**

COMB JELLIES — jellyfishlike; no stinging cells; some with paired tentacles. **53**

WORMS — six groups (phyla), with distinct characteristics; some round, some flat, some segmented. **54-57**

TO SEASHORE LIFE

BRYOZOANS and LAMP SHELLS — small, diverse, and ancient groups. **58-59**

STARFISH and KIN (6,000 species) — with radial bodies (five divisions). **60-66**

ARTHROPODS — jointed-legged, with external skeleton; a vast group. **67-79**

> **Crustacea** (25,000 species) — jointed legs and segmented abdomens; includes barnacles, crabs, lobsters, shrimp. **68-79**

MOLLUSKS or SHELLFISH (80,000 species) — soft-bodied, shelled. **80-140**

> **Chitons** — primitive mollusks with 8-plated shell. **81**

> **Bivalves** (Pelecypods) — animals with shell in two lateral halves. **82-110**

> **Univalves** (Gastropods) — animals with single coiled shell or no visible shell. **111-137**

> **Squids, Octopuses, and Kin** — well-developed head with tentacles; usually no external shell. **138-139**

> **Tusk or Tooth Shells** — a small group with tusklike shells. **140**

BIRDS — of the 70,000 species of vertebrates, including sharks and fish, whales and other marine mammals, only shore birds are covered in this book. **147-153**

ACTIVITIES FOR AMATEURS

OBSERVATION is the key to science and to enjoying shore life. Watch carefully; details of form and movement cannot be seen otherwise. Observe at the beach. Take live specimens home for study. Make a salt-water aquarium in which to keep small specimens alive. The practice of keeping notes and records will make your observations sharper, your understanding broader.

CLOTHING is important in your ventures—warm clothing and rubber boots in colder months, a bathing suit or the equivalent at other times. Wear sneakers to protect feet. Goggles and snorkels will give experienced swimmers entrée into a new world. Beginners be careful!

EQUIPMENT can be simple. Use binoculars for birds, a pail and other wide-mouthed containers for algae and small animals. A trowel, a spading fork, and a kitchen or putty knife are handy. Later you may find landing and dredging nets a help; with them, collecting from a small boat is rewarding fun. A good magnifying glass or, better still, a low-power microscope will give you a chance to study small invertebrates while they sport in a few tablespoons of sea water. For preserving sea animals, use rubbing alcohol, slightly diluted. Mollusks can be cleaned by boiling. Starfish and kin can be dried in the sun.

VISIT different types of shores. Note the variation in the kinds of life on mud flats, sandy beaches, and rocky shores, and determine the reasons for the different adaptations. Dig into the sand and the mud. Look under the rocks. Wade out, especially at low tide, to see what you might otherwise miss. Don't overlook the algae and shells washed ashore after storms. Some smaller creatures are most interesting and attractive when examined closely.

GET HELP in identifying your specimens. In addition to this book, try those listed on p. 154. At your library you will find more, including technical journals and special government reports. Experts at museums can give assistance. Dealers in shells may help you in identification and can also supply specimens for your collection.

SHORES ARE FRAGILE Estuaries, marshes, and other coastal shallows are the breeding grounds and nurseries for much of the life in the sea. They are a rich resource, and the life they support is fed basically from nutrients washed in from the land. Everyone who enjoys the wind and the tide, the terns, the shells underfoot, and all that lives in the sea beyond has a stake in maintaining the shores in their natural state.

Pollution of shore waters by ships, cities, factories, and farms is a serious problem. Chemical wastes can kill directly or can lower the oxygen content so that life can no longer survive. Dredging for marinas, canals, and ports, and draining for developments and for agriculture are responsible for most losses of valuable seashore.

Observe and enjoy life along the shores. You become literally an ecologist—someone who studies how different kinds of life are interrelated and dependent on each other. With your appreciation of seashores spawned, you become also a conservationist.

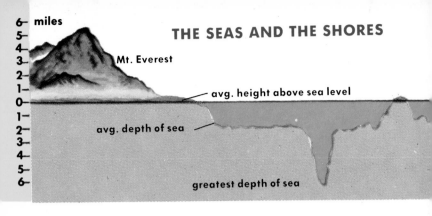

THE SEAS AND THE SHORES

miles
6
5
4
3 — Mt. Everest
2
1
0 — avg. height above sea level
1
2 — avg. depth of sea
3
4
5
6 — greatest depth of sea

THE SEAS cover about 72% of the earth's surface—61% of the Northern and 81% of the Southern hemisphere. The average height of all the land is about ½ mile. If the surface of the earth were smooth, an ocean 2 miles deep would cover it. The weight of the seas in tons is estimated at the figure 12 followed by 17 zeros. This water, a great reservoir of heat, profoundly affects climate. Dissolved in it are oxygen, carbon dioxide, and other gases; so are many solids, which make up about 3½% of the weight of the seas. These solids include more gold than has ever been mined and enough iron to last man thousands of years. The United States alone has 88,600 miles of coastline; the world, probably over a million. Shores are rich with life, and here important geologic changes are taking place.

Seas cover nearly ¾ of the earth's surface.

Graptolites (enlarged)

Shallow-water life about 400 million years ago

LIFE existed in the seas for millions of years before venturing onto land. The transition was a slow one, and the shore zone was a critical area in the process. Some ancient sea animals have survived and have changed so little they closely resemble their fossil ancestors; others changed greatly. But land animals still show traces of their origins. The liquid portion of your blood and also the blood of other land animals contains in solution many of the same chemicals as sea water.

SINKING SHORELINE

Arch

Sea cliffs

Rocky beach

Wave-cut terrace

SEASHORES are the battle line between land and sea. In some places, the sea carves the land into sea cliffs, terraces, arches, caves, and rocky beaches. These dramatic shores and headlands may encompass shallow bays where sand and pebbles form protected beaches. A wealth of life is often found on rocks between the tidemarks. Tide pools are unique places to study shore life.

In other places, large areas of sloping sea bottom are exposed. Sand, moved by waves and currents, builds up

an offshore bar or barrier beach between a protected lagoon and the breakers. Bars and spits also develop. Wind moves dry sand into shifting dunes. Brackish tidal marshes may form with abundant plants, birds, and smaller animals. Life along sandy beaches is distinct from life on rocky shores. Different kinds of shellfish, worms, and crustaceans live on each. Sandy beaches may appear quite barren, except for things washed up, but tiny forms of life may exist in films of water covering each grain of sand.

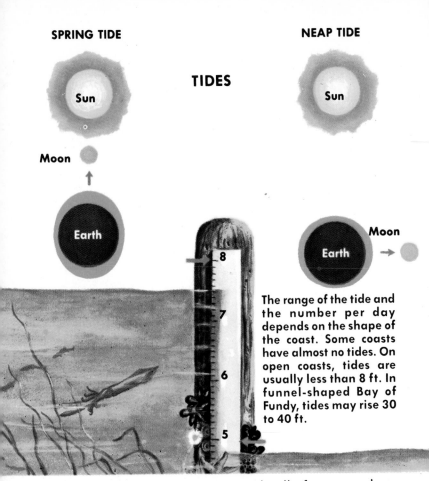

SPRING TIDE

NEAP TIDE

TIDES

Sun

Moon

Earth

Sun

Earth

Moon

The range of the tide and the number per day depends on the shape of the coast. Some coasts have almost no tides. On open coasts, tides are usually less than 8 ft. In funnel-shaped Bay of Fundy, tides may rise 30 to 40 ft.

TIDES result from the gravitational pull of moon and sun. The moon, much nearer the earth, has a stronger pull than the sun. When sun and moon are in line with earth and pull together, high tide is highest, low tide lowest. When they pull at a right angle, tides are less extreme. As the moon revolves and the earth turns, the tidal bulge moves around the earth. Tides on the Atlantic and Pacific coasts come about an hour later each day. Shapes of the ocean basin and of the coasts affect tides. The Gulf of Mexico has 1- or 2-ft. tides; elsewhere they are 4 to 8 ft. or more.

wind

AT SEA

WAVES are caused by the winds. The steady push of wind gives the water its rolling, rising and falling motion. As the water moves up and down, the wave itself moves forward. Waves have little effect a hundred feet down, but as they move into shallow water near the shore, the friction of the bottom causes them to rise higher until they tip forward in an arc and break. The breaker, like a miniature waterfall, rushes up the beach until its energy is exhausted. Currents along the shores may be set up by wave action.

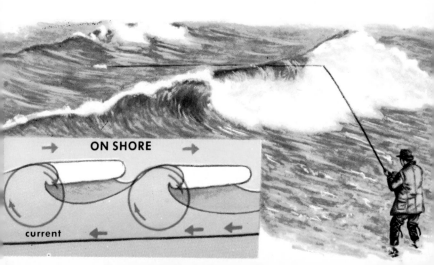

ON SHORE

current

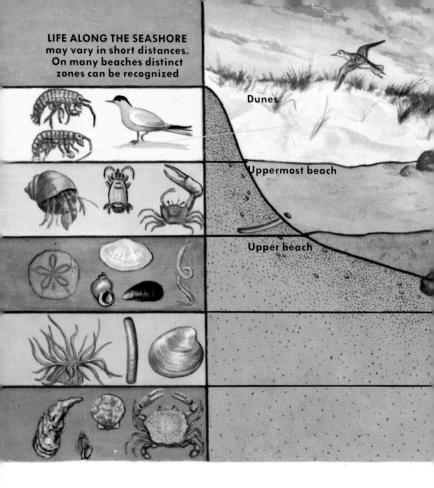

LIFE ALONG THE SEASHORE may vary in short distances. On many beaches distinct zones can be recognized

Dunes

Uppermost beach

Upper beach

SHORE LIFE differs on rocky and sandy beaches and on exposed and protected ones. Many beaches are divided into broad life zones.

First and highest is the dry beach or dune area. The uppermost beach is reached only by the highest tides, storm waves, and ocean spray. The upper beach gets wet by tides twice daily, but the plants and animals there are more adapted to land and air than to water. In the middle beach, which is covered with water most of the time, living things are normally less exposed to the air and are

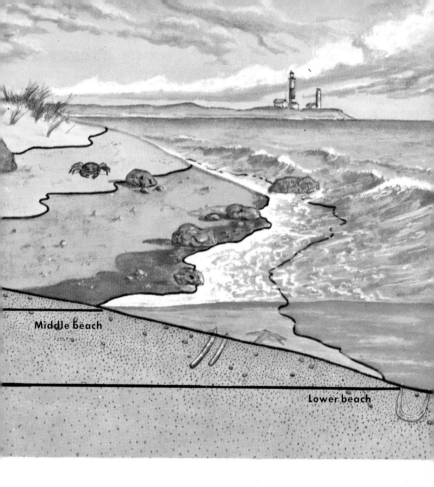

Middle beach

Lower beach

more harmed by drying. The lower beach is almost always submerged except during the very lowest tides and so is exposed no more than twice monthly—during the "spring" tides.

Living things form characteristic communities within these broad zones. Each kind of life is adapted to a particular marine environment and its food supply. Water temperature due to latitude or offshore currents, salinity as affected by streams, and pollution from ships and cities modify the shore life of a region.

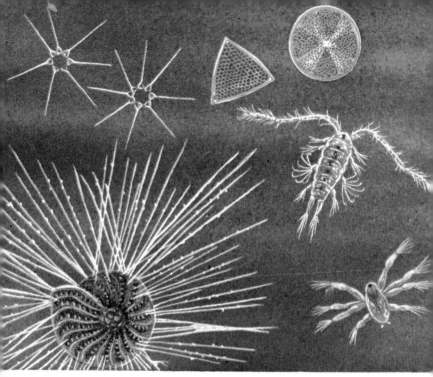

Foraminifera   Diatoms (top)   Copepods

PLANKTON is to the sea what grass is to the land—the basic food. All forms of plankton are very small, often microscopic. Billions upon billions live in the sea. In colder waters diatoms supply almost nine-tenths of the food. They are the most abundant of the plankton, but others, including dinoflagellates, are also primary producers of food. Among the many kinds of plankton animals, which include larval or immature stages of numerous animals, are copepods—tiny relatives of lobsters and crabs. Plankton serves

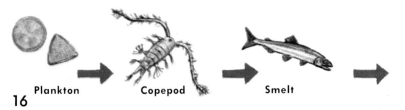

Plankton   Copepod   Smelt

Dinoflagellates   Radiolarians

as food for small fish and other sea animals which, in turn, are eaten by larger species. One authority figures about 10,000 lb. of diatoms are eaten to make 1,000 lb. of copepods, and 1,000 lb. of copepods produce 100 lb. of smelts. The 100 lb. of smelts, when eaten, give 10 lb. of mackerel which, as food, make 1 lb. of tuna. Caught, canned, and eaten, 1 lb. of tuna increases man's body weight by only 0.1 lb. Such food chains illustrate the interdependence of sea life.

Mackerel   Tuna

MARINE ALGAE

Seaweeds, or marine algae, are easy to collect, preserve, and study. Of about 18,000 kinds of algae, some live on land, more in fresh water, but most are marine. These grow attached to rocks, piles, and even boats. Storms wash up deep-water species. Any rocky beach or wharf is good collecting ground. Take a pail, spoon, knife, and putty knife along. Wear appropriate clothing. Scrape algae free and drop them into your pail of sea water. Later, at home, float one at a time in a large tray or dishpan. As it floats, arrange, trim, and spread it. Slip a sheet of heavy white paper under it. Raise slowly, letting it settle and the water drain off. Most smaller specimens will adhere and dry in place. Larger seaweeds can be photographed, or they can be preserved in alcohol or 6% formaldehyde. Most interesting is studying the algae while they are still alive. To do this, you need a microscope and much patience.

2. Float specimen into position. Raise paper and remove slowly.

1. Float specimen in pan of sea water. Slide heavy paper beneath.

3. Cover with cheese-cloth. Dry between blotters, mount, and label.

Mermaid's Hair

BLUE-GREEN ALGAE are a widespread group of some 1,500 inconspicuous species, both marine and fresh-water. They form dark scums on mud, rocks, and piles, or appear as a velvety fuzz on boat bottoms. Most are dark bluish-green in color and can thrive in polluted waters unsuited for other algae and animal life. Some species live in hot springs; others give the Red Sea its color. Identification is difficult without microscopic examination of the threadlike, often gelatinous growths. Mermaid's Hair lives on mud, rocks, and piling in shallow water of both coasts. The simple, unbranched filaments are curled and matted.

GREEN ALGAE, including over 5,000 species, are more common in fresh water and on moist soil than in the sea. Marine species are found along all shores but are more abundant in warmer waters. These are smaller and more delicate than the great kelps, and prefer more shallow water. Some green algae are single cells. Better-known marine species grow as filaments, irregular sheets, or branching fronds. Some tropical species take lime from sea water and help build "coral" reefs. No algae have roots, stems, or leaves like higher plants. Blue-green algae have no specialized sex cells; reproduction is vegetative, cells splitting off to form new growths. In the green algae, sex cells are formed, though vegetative reproduction also is common in nearly all species.

CODIUM, a very common and widely distributed marine green alga, occurs along the Atlantic, Gulf, and Pacific coasts. Sometimes called Sponge Seaweed because of its soft, spongelike texture, Codium has many branching stalks. It is closely related to Sea Moss or Bryopsis, described on p. 23.

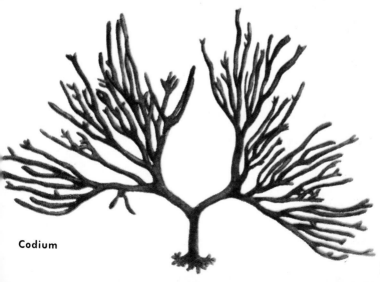

Codium

CLADOPHORA is a group of variable species, quite common on the North Atlantic Coast. Vary from silky, compact, green tufts to coarser filaments that may be 3 to 12 in. long.

3a

ENTEROMORPHA, 4 in. to 2 ft. long, often called "grass," is a common green alga of rocks, tidal pools, piers, and boat bottoms. Some species are stringy or ribbonlike, others flattened, thickened, or with inflated branches.

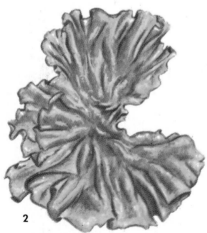

SEA LETTUCE, or Ulva, is common on both coasts. Largest of the green algae, to 3 ft. long, it is sheet- or ribbonlike. A number of species, typical of shallows, grow on rocks or in mud flats.

3b

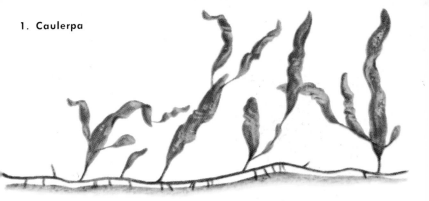

1. Caulerpa

CAULERPA is common on sandy and muddy bottoms in warm water and on coral reefs. It spreads by horizontal stems, covering large areas. Fronds, 2 to 4 in. long, are eaten by sea turtles. Variable in form—some with simple fronds, some branched.

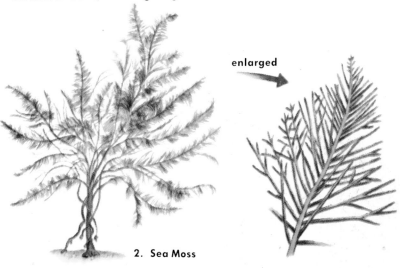

enlarged

2. Sea Moss

SEA MOSS or Bryopsis includes some 20 species. All branch and rebranch, giving them a delicate and feathery appearance. Sea Moss is abundant along the entire coasts of the Atlantic and the Pacific, growing on rocks and piers and occasionally in mud. Grows 2 to 8 in. long and is a darker green than other green algae. Species of Sea Moss are marked by differences in branching and fineness of the filaments. Sea Moss tends to grow in most abundance where there is a seepage of fresh water from the shore into the sea.

23

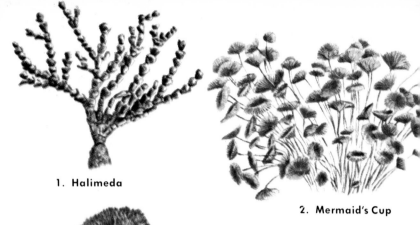

1. Halimeda

2. Mermaid's Cup

3. Merman's Shaving Brush

TROPICAL GREEN ALGAE are more common than cold-water species. Along the warmer parts of the Atlantic and Gulf coasts are several species, small in size and unusual in form. Merman's Shaving Brush (*Penicillus*), 2 to 5 in. long, is shaped true to its name. Several species of Halimeda have unusual thin, roundish, branching segments, their growth cactuslike. Mermaid's Cup (*Acetabularia*), 1 to 3 in. tall, is like a small, greenish-white mushroom. Patches of these three algae may carpet shallow areas.

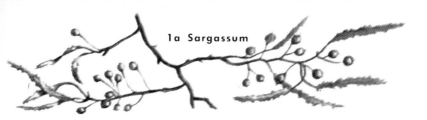

1a Sargassum

BROWN ALGAE include, in the 1,000 or so kinds known, some of the largest and most interesting algae. Brown algae are diverse in form and structure; some have involved life histories. They reproduce vegetatively and by the union of male and female cells, which swim out into the water. All brown algae contain a greenish-brown pigment that absorbs light like the green pigment of green algae. This pigment is effective at medium depths, so brown algae may grow at depths of 75 ft. Tremendous beds of brown algae stretch along temperate and cooler shores. These algae are used for fertilizer and as a source of iodine and potash. The chemical algin, made from them, is used to make puddings smoother, to finish paper, to apply dyes and inks, and in medicine.

SARGASSUM, most famous of the brown algae, floats over mile after mile in the "Sargasso Sea" of the Atlantic. Over 150 species, most of them to 3 ft. or longer, occur widely in warmer waters, but some are found well to the north on our Atlantic and Pacific coasts. Fronds outwardly resemble stems and leaves; air bladders of varying size are common.

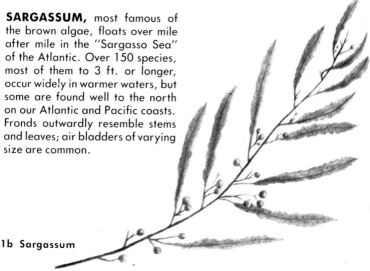

1b Sargassum

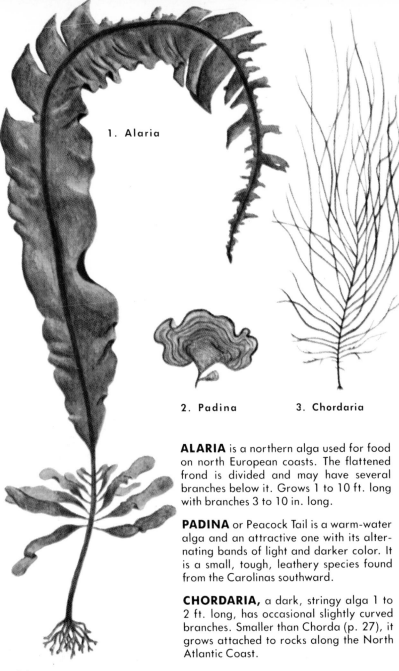

1. Alaria

2. Padina

3. Chordaria

ALARIA is a northern alga used for food on north European coasts. The flattened frond is divided and may have several branches below it. Grows 1 to 10 ft. long with branches 3 to 10 in. long.

PADINA or Peacock Tail is a warm-water alga and an attractive one with its alternating bands of light and darker color. It is a small, tough, leathery species found from the Carolinas southward.

CHORDARIA, a dark, stringy alga 1 to 2 ft. long, has occasional slightly curved branches. Smaller than Chorda (p. 27), it grows attached to rocks along the North Atlantic Coast.

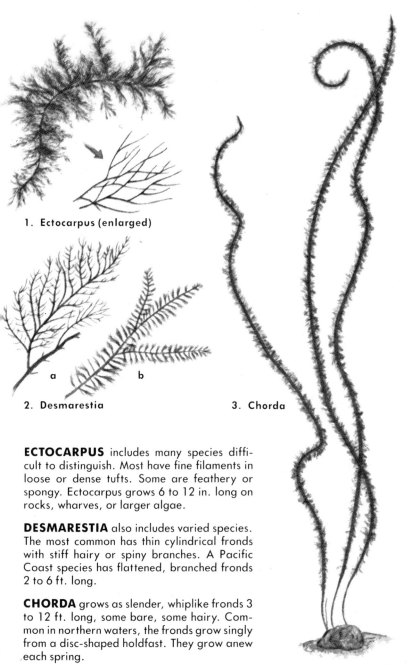

1. Ectocarpus (enlarged)

2. Desmarestia

a   b

3. Chorda

ECTOCARPUS includes many species difficult to distinguish. Most have fine filaments in loose or dense tufts. Some are feathery or spongy. Ectocarpus grows 6 to 12 in. long on rocks, wharves, or larger algae.

DESMARESTIA also includes varied species. The most common has thin cylindrical fronds with stiff hairy or spiny branches. A Pacific Coast species has flattened, branched fronds 2 to 6 ft. long.

CHORDA grows as slender, whiplike fronds 3 to 12 ft. long, some bare, some hairy. Common in northern waters, the fronds grow singly from a disc-shaped holdfast. They grow anew each spring.

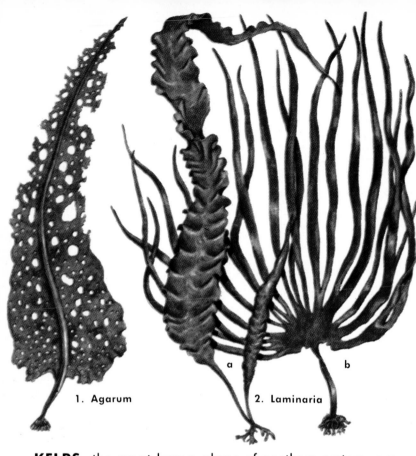

1. Agarum   a   2. Laminaria   b

KELPS, the great brown algae of northern waters, are harvested on the Pacific Coast, and thousands of tons are used yearly in chemical industries. In Asian waters, these algae are "farmed" for food. East Coast kelps include Alaria (p. 26), Laminaria, and Agarum. West Coast kelps are larger and more imposing; some grow to lengths of over 100 ft. A tough holdfast anchors the kelps to the rocky bottom; air bladders float the plant to the surface. Kelps grow from the low-tide mark to depths of 100 ft. or more. Nereocystis and Macrocystis include the largest and best-known Pacific species. Sea Palm (*Postelsia*) is one of the most unusual looking of all marine algae.

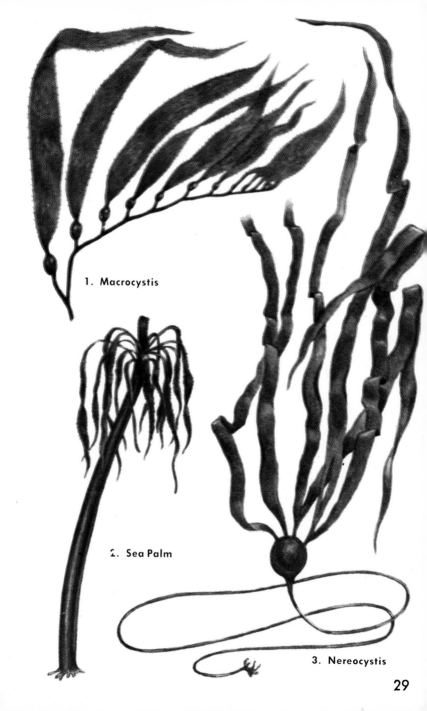

1. Macrocystis

2. Sea Palm

3. Nereocystis

29

FUCUS or Rockweed is a large brown alga and one of the most widely distributed seaweeds. It abounds on all cool, rocky shores. A number of species have swollen air bladders along the midrib and are similar in structure and habit. The life history of Fucus is an example of how seaweeds grow and reproduce. Parts of Fucus, torn loose by waves, continue to grow and may become established as new growths; otherwise, they reproduce by specialized cells. Other brown algae have similar methods of reproduction. Where Fucus grows abundantly, it sometimes washes ashore in heaps or is easily raked from the shallows. It is then dried in the sun and spread over fields as fertilizer, adding not only gross organic matter but also valuable minerals from the sea.

1a

1b

RED ALGAE are admirable for delicate color and form. Most of the 2,500 kinds prefer deeper waters than do other algae. Their red pigment absorbs more blue and violet light that penetrates deepest in the ocean, and so red algae can manufacture food at depths of 100 to 200 ft. Species living closer to shore are important in tidal pool life. Some lack the typical delicate branching pattern and are coarse, flattened, or clublike.

Several species when boiled yield agar-agar, valuable in medicine and bacteriology. In the Orient, British Isles, and Scandinavia, other red algae—Irish moss, dulse, laver, slack—are widely used as food or for chemicals. Field identification of most red algae is difficult.

DASYA is found from Florida to Cape Cod. The delicate orange-brown to red-purple fronds, with many thin, hairy branches, are 6 in. to 3 ft. long. Look on shells and rocks in quiet, protected areas below the low-tide mark. When taken from the water, the fragile, delicate fronds collapse into a red or purple jellylike mass. Dasya is a large and well-known genus. A number of species are found also on rocks along the Pacific Coast.

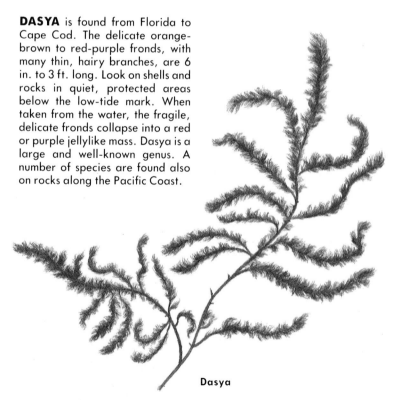

Dasya

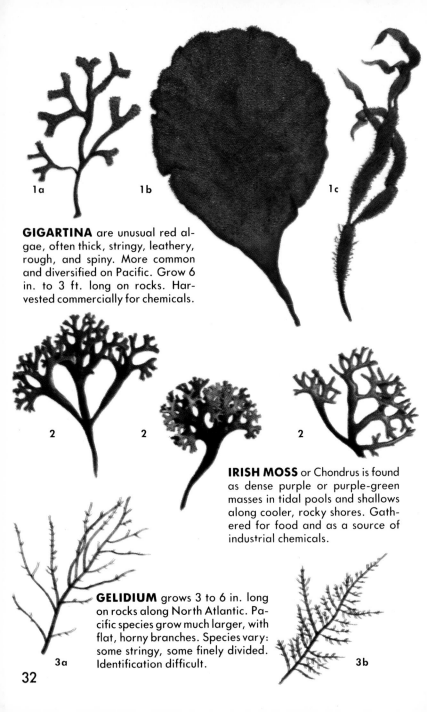

GIGARTINA are unusual red algae, often thick, stringy, leathery, rough, and spiny. More common and diversified on Pacific. Grow 6 in. to 3 ft. long on rocks. Harvested commercially for chemicals.

1a 1b 1c

2 2 2

IRISH MOSS or Chondrus is found as dense purple or purple-green masses in tidal pools and shallows along cooler, rocky shores. Gathered for food and as a source of industrial chemicals.

GELIDIUM grows 3 to 6 in. long on rocks along North Atlantic. Pacific species grow much larger, with flat, horny branches. Species vary: some stringy, some finely divided. Identification difficult.

3a 3b

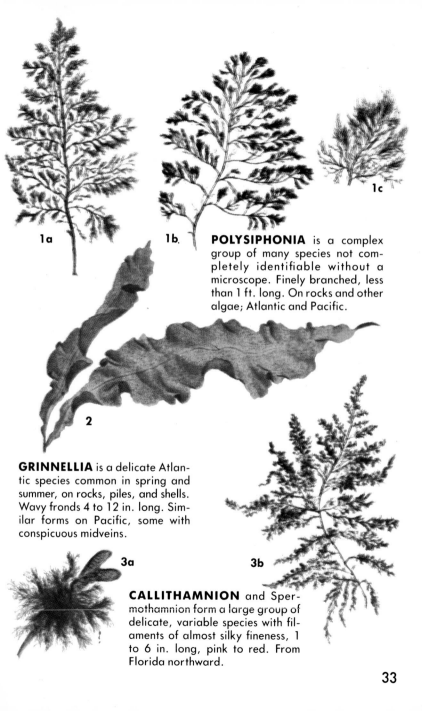

POLYSIPHONIA is a complex group of many species not completely identifiable without a microscope. Finely branched, less than 1 ft. long. On rocks and other algae; Atlantic and Pacific.

1a

1b.

1c

2

GRINNELLIA is a delicate Atlantic species common in spring and summer, on rocks, piles, and shells. Wavy fronds 4 to 12 in. long. Similar forms on Pacific, some with conspicuous midveins.

3a

3b

CALLITHAMNION and Spermothamnion form a large group of delicate, variable species with filaments of almost silky fineness, 1 to 6 in. long, pink to red. From Florida northward.

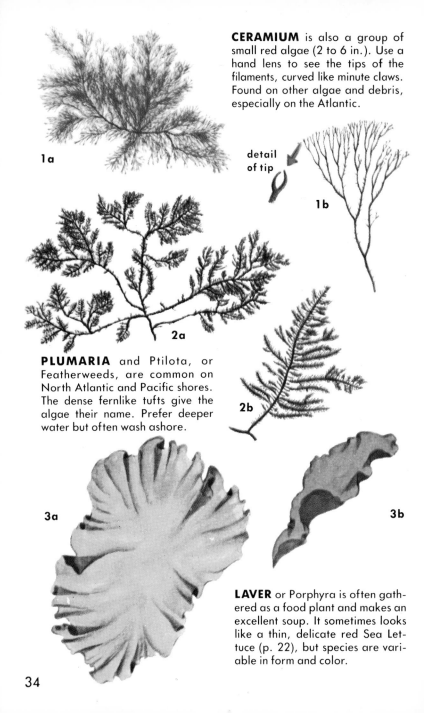

CERAMIUM is also a group of small red algae (2 to 6 in.). Use a hand lens to see the tips of the filaments, curved like minute claws. Found on other algae and debris, especially on the Atlantic.

1a

detail of tip

1b

2a

PLUMARIA and Ptilota, or Featherweeds, are common on North Atlantic and Pacific shores. The dense fernlike tufts give the algae their name. Prefer deeper water but often wash ashore.

2b

3a

3b

LAVER or Porphyra is often gathered as a food plant and makes an excellent soup. It sometimes looks like a thin, delicate red Sea Lettuce (p. 22), but species are variable in form and color.

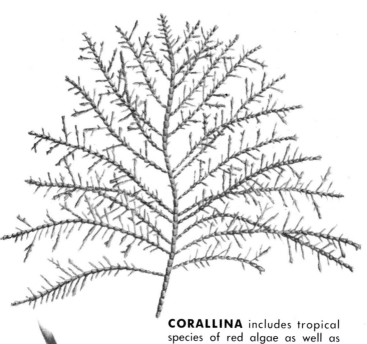

detail
of frond

CORALLINA includes tropical species of red algae as well as some that grow far north into Canadian waters. Others are found along the Pacific Coast. Corallinas are slender, rarely more than 3 inches tall, and bushy, the branches always opposite. At the joints they are round, but above the joints they are flattened or wedge-shaped. Most are reddish-purple, a few species grayish-green. When they are washed up on shore, the sun quickly bleaches them into chalky white.

The ability of these algae to extract lime from sea water and deposit it as an encrustation is shared with some green algae (p. 24). These algae contribute greatly to the building of coral reefs.

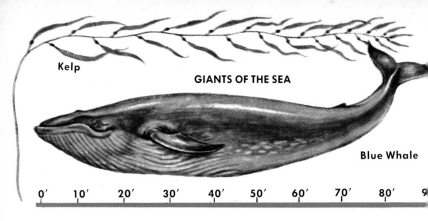

Kelp

GIANTS OF THE SEA

Blue Whale

0'   10'   20'   30'   40'   50'   60'   70'   80'   9

LIFE IN THE SEA is distributed in complex and interdependent patterns. The range in size of ocean organisms is tremendous—from bacteria 1/25,000 in. long to giant kelps (p. 28) that grow to more than 100 ft. The span in length in the marine animals is about the same, but the much greater range in weight is hard to imagine. Marine protozoa weigh as little as 1/6,000,000,000,000,000 oz. The great Blue Whale weighs up to 150 tons—or 21,800,000,000,000,000,000 times as much.

Both the large and the small are bound together by their water environment, and even more tightly into living communities within the seas. Such communities are very evident along the shore. Anyone who begins to study shore life will find obvious signs of them. The intensive study of such communities may yield more knowledge of interdependence and greater satisfaction than the accumulation of many shells.

MICROSCOPIC SEA LIFE

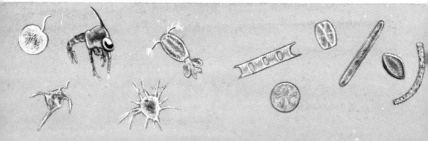

Pacific Coast tidal pool

SEASHORE COMMUNITIES are determined by such things as the nature of the shore—rocky, sandy, or muddy. The depth of water or the range in tides is another factor; so are currents, the temperature of the water, and dilution from fresh-water streams. These factors, working together, enable some groups of living things to survive and develop into communities. Food is supplied by the primary producers, mostly plankton. Larger animals feed on smaller organisms. Others feed on decaying organic matter. Some sea animals can exist in a wide range of surroundings and are found along most shores. Others are highly selective. These conditions make the difference between a Pacific Coast protected tidal pool and the clam-rich mud flats of Long Island Sound.

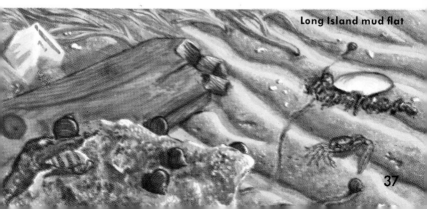

Long Island mud flat

37

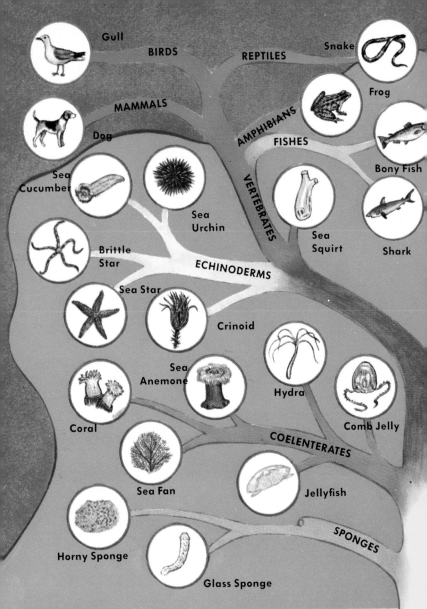

Gull

BIRDS

REPTILES

Snake

MAMMALS

Frog

AMPHIBIANS

Dog

FISHES

Sea Cucumber

VERTEBRATES

Sea Urchin

Brittle Star

ECHINODERMS

Sea Squirt

Shark

Bony Fish

Sea Star

Crinoid

Sea Anemone

Hydra

Coral

Comb Jelly

COELENTERATES

Sea Fan

Jellyfish

SPONGES

Horny Sponge

Glass Sponge

ANIMALS OF THE SEA and of the land are one. Nearly every major group of animals includes kinds that are adapted to sea life. All the animals in each group are

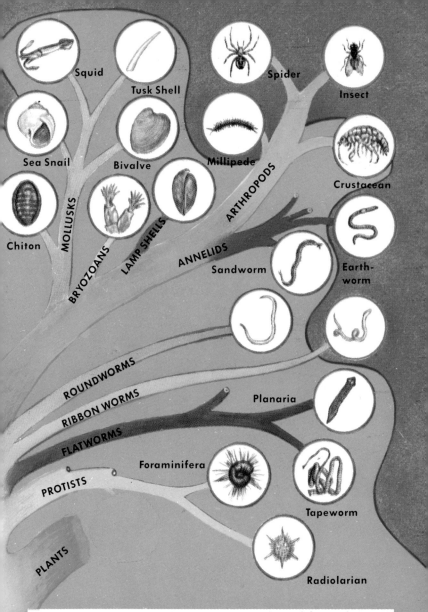

Squid

Tusk Shell

Spider

Insect

Sea Snail

Bivalve

Millipede

Crustacean

Chiton

MOLLUSKS

BRYOZOANS

LAMP SHELLS

ARTHROPODS

ANNELIDS

Sandworm

Earthworm

ROUNDWORMS

RIBBON WORMS

Planaria

FLATWORMS

Foraminifera

PROTISTS

Tapeworm

PLANTS

Radiolarian

related to one another and have developed from common ancestors. The "family tree" of animal life shown above is a general picture of their relationship.

SEA SQUIRTS (Ascidians) These oddly formed animals, such as Ciona and Sea Grapes, have the hint of a backbone. They grow on rocks and piling.

1. Ciona   2. Sea Grapes

FAMILY TREE OF ANIMAL LIFE

At the base of the family tree of animal life are sponges, which live in warm, shallow seas as they did many millions of years ago. Sponges are simple or colonial animals. Some kinds, of ancient origin, have "skeletons" of silica; many have the fibrous (spongin) skeletons we all know. Jellyfish and hydroids are a large, complex, and diverse group—some solitary, some colonial. Coral animals build hard, limy walls that gradually make coral rock. The worms, though they look somewhat similar, differ greatly internally and hence are put into several distinct but related groups. Starfish and other echinoderms have a peculiar radial pattern of growth and unusual adaptations both for feeding and for moving.

Best known of shore animals are the mollusks. Collectors seek their many, varied shells. The living animals (some of which lack shells) are interesting, too. Detailed identification of shells may require more advanced books (p. 154) or the help of an expert. The arthropods or jointed-legged animals include such marine groups as crabs, lobsters, and barnacles. Along the shores we also find simple chordates—creatures related to ancestors of backboned animals, and we see shore birds (pp. 147-153) and fishes.

1. Leucosolenia

2. Grantia

LIME SPONGES are the simplest sponges. Some are single "urns"; others grow in colonies. Between the two cell walls are scattered needles (spicules) of lime that support the sponge and give the group its name. Water enters through pores in the sides and leaves through the opening at the top. The yellowish or gray Grantia (1 in. long) is found singly or in clusters on shells, rocks, or pilings. Some Leucosolenia are similar but smaller, growing in soft, yellowish mats. Other branching forms may grow to be an inch or so long.

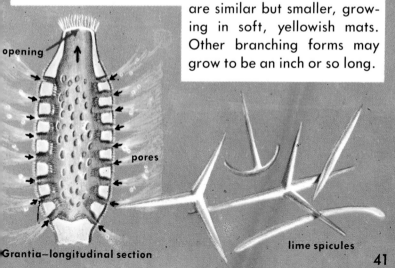

opening

pores

Grantia—longitudinal section

lime spicules

41

HORNY SPONGES, the best-known kinds, include over 2,000 species. A few live in ponds but most are marine, and common in warmer waters. A boring sponge, Cliona riddles shellfish with tiny holes. Suberites, the Sulfur Sponge, also attaches itself to shells and rocks where it grows 2 to 3 in. long. Both are shallow-water species. Microciona, or Redbeard Sponge, encrusts shells and pilings. Similar orange and yellow species occur on Atlantic and Pacific coasts. Deadman's Fingers is commonly washed up on beaches.

Sponge diver

1. Redbeard Sponge

2. Boring Sponge

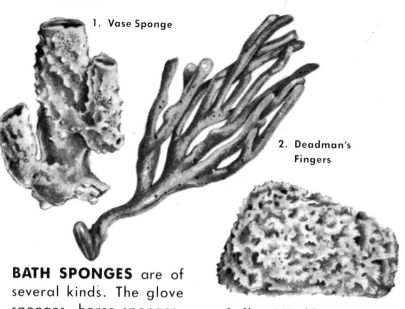

1. Vase Sponge

2. Deadman's Fingers

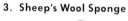
3. Sheep's Wool Sponge

4. Glove Sponge

5. Grass Sponge

BATH SPONGES are of several kinds. The glove sponges, horse sponges, and sheep's wool sponges are gathered by divers. They are dried, cleaned, and bleached before they are sold. The once-important American sponge fishing industry, centered at Tarpon Springs, Florida, has given way to artificial sponges made of cellulose. Vase sponges, grass sponges, and dozens of other kinds of sponges are found in Gulf waters, growing on the ocean bottom and feeding on small organisms. Sponges can regrow lost or injured parts.

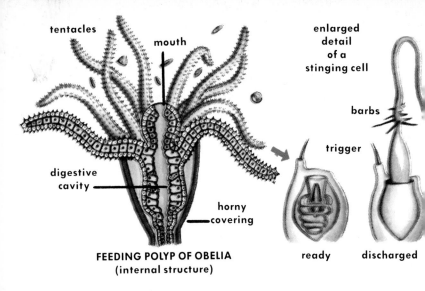

tentacles

mouth

enlarged detail of a stinging cell

barbs

trigger

digestive cavity

horny covering

FEEDING POLYP OF OBELIA
(internal structure)

ready   discharged

POLYP and JELLYFISH ANIMALS (Coelenterates), a diverse group, have a central digestive cavity. Its opening is ringed by stinging tentacles that stun or kill small prey. Many have both a free-swimming (medusa or jellyfish) and a more fixed (polyp or hydroid) stage. Some are colonial. Coelenterates include Hydrozoa (polyps and medusae, usually small); Scyphozoa (medusae only, fairly large); and Anthozoa (polyps only, usually fairly large).

THREE MAJOR GROUPS OF COELENTERATES

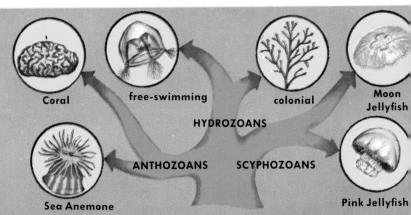

Coral

free-swimming

colonial

Moon Jellyfish

HYDROZOANS

Sea Anemone

ANTHOZOANS   **SCYPHOZOANS**

Pink Jellyfish

1. **Moon Jellyfish** 3"-9"　　　　　2. **Pink Jellyfish** 1'-8'

MOON JELLYFISH, very common and washing up on all our beaches, varies in color from white to pink and orange. Its milky disc has radiating canals and a thin indented fringe. Tentacles are very short. Pink Jellyfish, of colder waters, is larger and has long, trailing tentacles. Specimens 8 ft. across with tentacles over 100 ft. long are reported. It swims by opening and closing its disc.

HYDROZOANS are of many kinds. Obelias are small colonies growing on rocks, piles, or seaweeds. Common along the Atlantic Coast, they are found the world over. Note the branching stems that under magnification show both feeding and reproductive polyps. The small, free-swimming medusae have 8 to 24 tentacles. Tubularia, unbranched or in small colonies, is most common in northern waters, but some are found as far south as Florida. Each hydroid (about ¼ in. or less in diameter) has about two dozen short tentacles. Gonionemus, a New England species, is typical of many free-swimming hydroids. It is about an inch in diameter, with 60 to 80 tentacles, each less than an

1. Gonionemus 1" diam.

2. Tubularia 1"-2" long

3. Obelia 1"-8" long

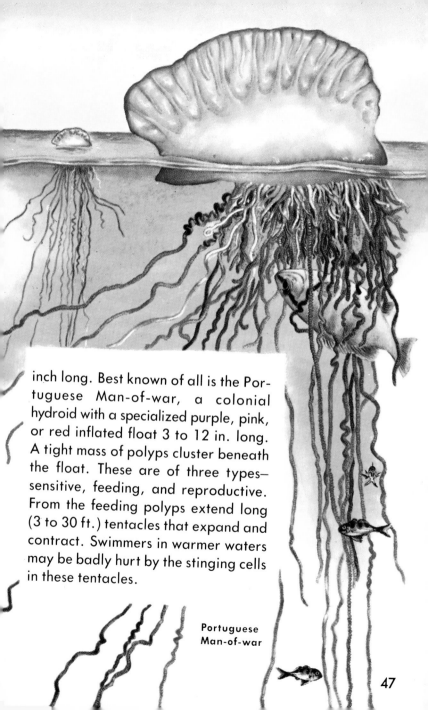

inch long. Best known of all is the Portuguese Man-of-war, a colonial hydroid with a specialized purple, pink, or red inflated float 3 to 12 in. long. A tight mass of polyps cluster beneath the float. These are of three types— sensitive, feeding, and reproductive. From the feeding polyps extend long (3 to 30 ft.) tentacles that expand and contract. Swimmers in warmer waters may be badly hurt by the stinging cells in these tentacles.

Portuguese
Man-of-war

47

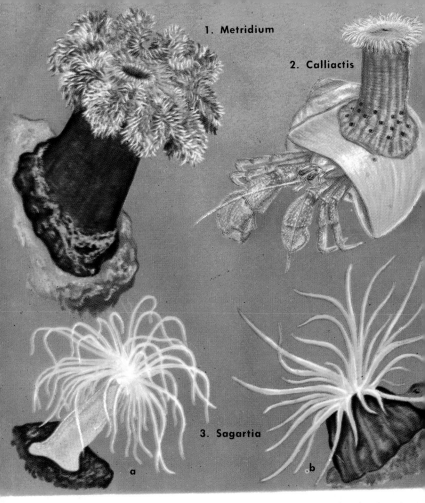

1. Metridium

2. Calliactis

3. Sagartia

a

b

SEA ANEMONES grow attached to rocks and piles and resemble flowers. The tentacles around the mouth cavity open like fleshy petals and contract whenever danger threatens. Sea anemones do not have a free-swimming jellyfish stage. The fertilized egg grows into a larva that soon settles down to a fixed existence. Metridium, sometimes 3 in. high, with many white tentacles, is common in northern waters, both Atlantic and Pacific. Several species of Sagartia, about 1 in. high and delicately colored, are also found on both coasts, growing on rocks or in sand near the low-tide mark. The Pacific species, believed to have been introduced with oysters from Japan, is small (½ in.), dark green with orange stripes. Calliactis, an unusual anemone, may grow 3 in. high. It attaches itself to a Hermit Crab's adopted shell (p. 73) and so gets free transportation. It is most common along the South Atlantic Coast. The Green Anemone occurs abundantly in western tidal pools. The color is due to algae that actually live in the anemone's tissues. Both the anemone and the algae benefit from this partnership.

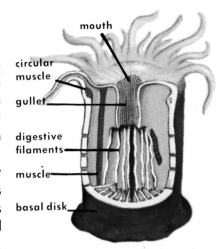

INTERNAL VIEW OF ANEMONE

mouth
circular muscle
gullet
digestive filaments
muscle
basal disk

Green Anemone

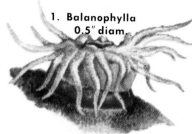

1. Balanophyllia
0.5" diam.

polyp expanded

top view of stony cup

2. Astrangia

Polyps 0.4" diam.

Astrangia skeleton

CORALS, closely related to sea anemones, are of several groups. One has bits of lime imbedded in the body walls but does not produce the typical coral "skeleton." Another (p. 52) makes horny skeletons. The stony corals are best known. These are the corals that form great reefs, atolls, and islands. Cells at the base of each polyp take lime from sea water to build up their skeletons. A few of these corals grow singly; most are colonial, thriving in warm, fairly shallow water. Northern species of corals are washed up on New England beaches, but most corals you will see come from South

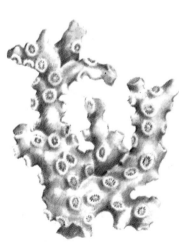

3. Oculina Coral skeleton

1. Precious Coral

beads

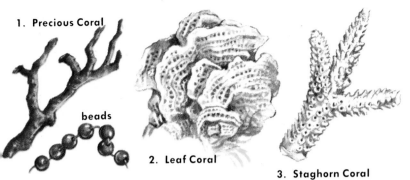

2. Leaf Coral

3. Staghorn Coral

4. Star Coral

Atlantic and Gulf waters. Two eastern, cooler-water corals are Astrangia and Oculina, both with white skeletons. The three Pacific kinds include Balanophylla, a solitary orange coral, and another Astrangia. Precious Coral comes from the Mediterranean. Similar species have recently been found in deep waters off California. About a dozen corals are common in Florida and West Indian reefs. All have white skeletons. Best known are Brain, Star, and Staghorn.

5. Brain Coral

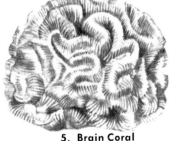

1. Sea Pen 4"

SEA FANS are horny corals, a group that also includes those called Sea Plumes or Sea Whips. Sea Fan is common in warmer waters on both coasts. Polyps are small, with eight tentacles. The flexible, brightly colored dried skeletons are often seen in curio shops.

The closely related Sea Pens were named for their unusual shape. Found in both Atlantic and Pacific, they grow from 4 in. to over a foot long. Muddy bottoms of some Pacific bays are covered with a common green Sea Pen. When disturbed these animals contract and seem to disappear.

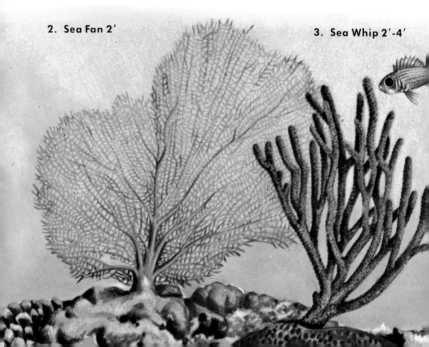

2. Sea Fan 2'

3. Sea Whip 2'-4'

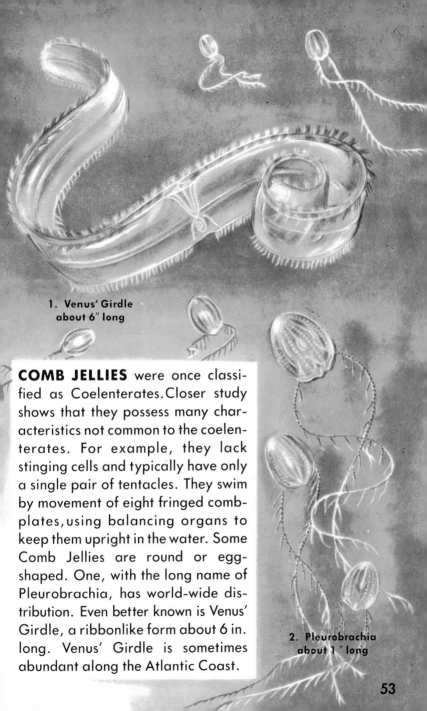

1. Venus' Girdle
about 6" long

COMB JELLIES were once classified as Coelenterates. Closer study
shows that they possess many characteristics not common to the coelenterates. For example, they lack
stinging cells and typically have only
a single pair of tentacles. They swim
by movement of eight fringed comb-
plates, using balancing organs to
keep them upright in the water. Some
Comb Jellies are round or egg-
shaped. One, with the long name of
Pleurobrachia, has world-wide dis-
tribution. Even better known is Venus'
Girdle, a ribbonlike form about 6 in.
long. Venus' Girdle is sometimes
abundant along the Atlantic Coast.

2. Pleurobrachia
about 1" long

53

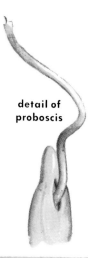

detail of proboscis

RIBBON WORMS, mostly marine, live in mud and under rocks by day, swimming at night. Ribbon worms are cylindrical or flat. Some are creamy, others red, orange, and purple. They range in length from 1 in. to nearly 90 ft. The largest in American waters may be 20 ft. long. Ribbon worms feed on small marine animals, capturing their food with a proboscis—a long tube with a pointed end. The proboscis can be shot out quickly to wrap around prey which is then drawn into the body.

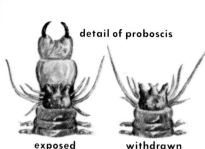

detail of proboscis

exposed   withdrawn

SANDWORMS belong to the group of segmented worms (pp. 56-57), the most advanced of the wormlike animals. Besides the segments, group characteristics include bristled appendages and internal organs arranged symmetrically. Sandworms are found in sand and under rocks along Atlantic and Pacific shorelines. They swim freely at night, especially during the breeding season. Other worms and small sea animals are seized by the sharp, horny jaws and eaten. A few species grow to several feet in length, but most are shorter. The omnivorous Clam Worm, illustrated here, is the best-known species, found on both eastern and western sides of the North Atlantic. It lives in a thin tube in sand or mud. Grows to a length of 12 to 18 in.

Males are bright blue-green. Females are duller with orange and red.

Clam Worm

55

Fan Worm

SEGMENTED WORMS, a group of some 8,000 species, include sandworms, leeches, and earthworms. The marine forms are varied, unusual, and may be brightly colored.

Sea Mouse is a broad worm covered with long, gray, iridescent "hair." It lives on sandy bottoms in shallow water on both sides of the North Atlantic. A related species has more prominent feeding appendages around the mouth.

Lugworm is a burrowing animal, like the earthworm. It lives well below the surface and feeds by extracting organic matter from the fine sand and debris taken in as it burrows.

Parchment Worms live in U-shaped tubes on muddy bottoms. Water sucked in at one end brings in oxygen and plankton food. Wastes are discharged at the other. The tube is built of a tough membrane, hence the common name of this worm. Tube openings can be seen dotting the bottom of shallow water at low tide.

Trumpet Worms are small segmented worms that build their conical tubes of grains of sand neatly and attractively cemented together. These sedentary animals use plumelike appendages for respiration and in gathering food, and curved ones to help them dig.

Fringed Worms are earthwormlike in appearance, except for the many long, thin, fleshy appendages growing from most segments. These are exposed and help the worm, which lives buried in the mud, obtain oxygen.

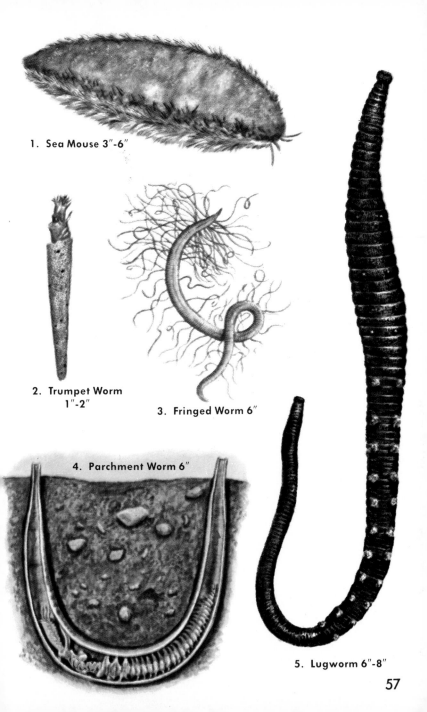

1. Sea Mouse 3″-6″

2. Trumpet Worm 1″-2″

3. Fringed Worm 6″

4. Parchment Worm 6″

5. Lugworm 6″-8″

57

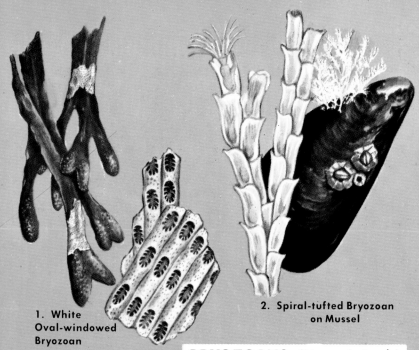

1. White
Oval-windowed
Bryozoan

2. Spiral-tufted Bryozoan
on Mussel

3. Bushy Gray Bryozoan

BRYOZOANS (Moss Animals) and Lamp Shells differ in appearance but belong to the same very ancient group of sea animals. Many fossils of both are found in rocks 250 to 500 million years old. Bryozoans are colonial. Individual animals are so small that a lens is needed to study them. Some build horny sheaths; some secrete lime like the corals. In each case the colony develops a distinctive pattern. Bryozoans feed on plankton. They are found in both shallow and deep water, on rocks, shells, debris, and seaweeds.

2. Southern Lamp Shell 0.5″

1. Northern Lamp Shell 0.8″

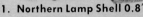

← interior

exterior →

3. Lingula about 1″

LAMP SHELLS, or Brachiopods, were once so common that thousands of fossil species have been found. By comparison, they are rare today. Living species often prefer deep water, but a few are found between the tides, attached to rocks by stalklike body projections. The animals have an upper and lower shell, while shells of bivalve mollusks are right and left. Internal structures show their close relationship to the bryozoans. Brachiopods feed on plankton, which they catch on fringelike appendages. Their size is small—from ½ to 2 in.

FAMILY TREE OF SPINY-SKINNED ANIMALS

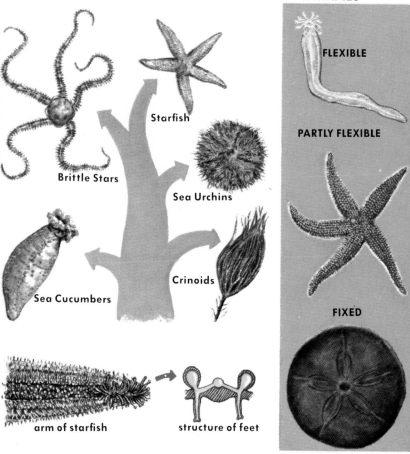

Brittle Stars

Starfish

Sea Urchins

Sea Cucumbers

Crinoids

FLEXIBLE

PARTLY FLEXIBLE

FIXED

arm of starfish

structure of feet

ECHINODERMS are marine animals that have limy plates, often with spines, for "skeletons." The plates may be connected at movable joints, as in some Starfish. They may form a continuous shell, as in the Sea Urchins, or they are not connected at all, as in Sea Cucumbers. Adult echinoderms exhibit a starlike pattern, some with radiating arms. Small tubefeet on these arms grip surfaces, helping the animal to move and obtain food. They connect to a system of internal tubes through which sea water circulates.

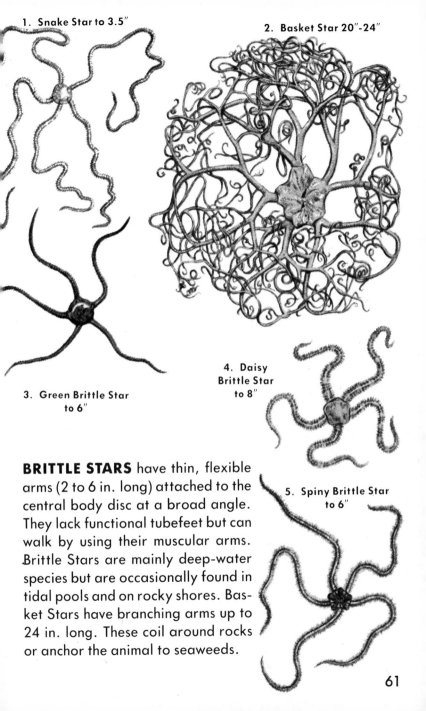

1. Snake Star to 3.5"

2. Basket Star 20"-24"

3. Green Brittle Star to 6"

4. Daisy Brittle Star to 8"

5. Spiny Brittle Star to 6"

BRITTLE STARS have thin, flexible arms (2 to 6 in. long) attached to the central body disc at a broad angle. They lack functional tubefeet but can walk by using their muscular arms. Brittle Stars are mainly deep-water species but are occasionally found in tidal pools and on rocky shores. Basket Stars have branching arms up to 24 in. long. These coil around rocks or anchor the animal to seaweeds.

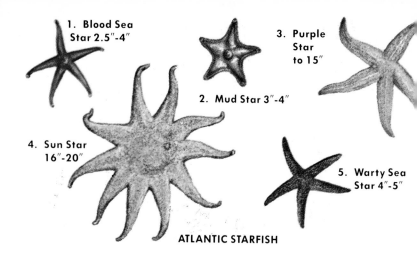

1. Blood Sea Star 2.5"-4"

2. Mud Star 3"-4"

3. Purple Star to 15"

4. Sun Star 16"-20"

5. Warty Sea Star 4"-5"

ATLANTIC STARFISH

STARFISH or SEA STARS are the best known of the echinoderms. Common Starfish have arms at a sharp angle to the central disc, which has on its top a sieve plate. Water enters this and then moves through tubes to the tubefeet in grooves located on the undersides of the arms.

6. Common or Eastern Starfish 6"-11"

PACIFIC STARFISH

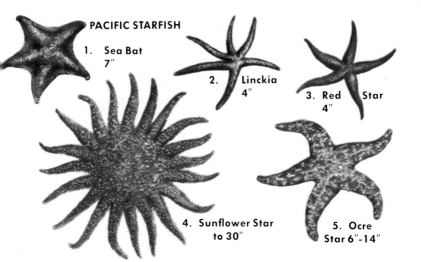

1. Sea Bat 7"
2. Linckia 4"
3. Red Star 4"
4. Sunflower Star to 30"
5. Ocre Star 6"-14"

Arms, 5 to 10 or more, vary with species; most are spiny, with very tiny pincers amid the spines. Underneath the disc is a mouth. Wrapping its arms over a clam, the starfish uses sustained suction of the tubefeet to pull it open. Then it extends its stomach through its mouth into the clam shell and digests the clam there. Starfish destroy millions of dollars' worth of shellfish yearly.

Common Starfish feeding on clam

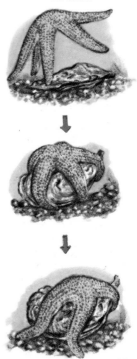

regeneration of arms

63

**1. Cidaris
to 2.5"**

SEA URCHINS are echinoderms in which the plates are joined to form a firm shell. A five-rayed pattern of pores for the tubefeet shows the close relationship to Starfish. Many Sea Urchins live on rocks in shallow water. Those that live in deeper water occur in groups and sometimes carpet a large area of sea bottom. Live Sea Urchins are covered with movable spines—long, short, delicate, or heavy, depending on the species. Those of some tropical species have around the base of the spines structures that extrude poison. Sea Urchin eggs are eaten in Europe and the West Indies. Sea Urchins range from 1½ to 10 in. in diameter.

SAND DOLLARS, sometimes called Sea Biscuits, are flattened relatives of the Sea Urchins with the movable spines greatly reduced in size. The animals live in deeper water, half-buried in sand, feeding on organic material and plankton. Cilia on the spines move these food particles until they are trapped by mucus around the spines and are pushed into the animal's mouth. A large Pacific starfish feeds on Sand Dollars. Sand Dollars and Sea Urchin "skeletons" are found washed up on beaches.

2. Purple Sea Urchin 1.5"-3"

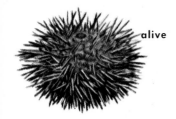

alive

dead

3. Sand Dollar 3"

alive

dea

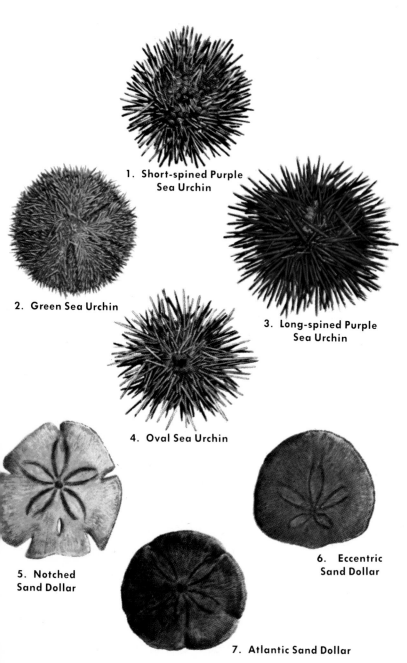

1. Short-spined Purple
   Sea Urchin

2. Green Sea Urchin

3. Long-spined Purple
   Sea Urchin

4. Oval Sea Urchin

5. Notched
   Sand Dollar

6. Eccentric
   Sand Dollar

7. Atlantic Sand Dollar

65

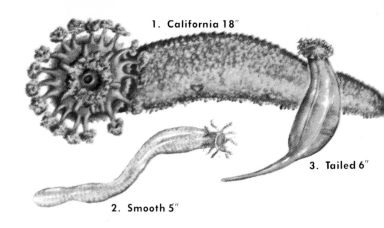

1. California 18"

3. Tailed 6"

2. Smooth 5"

SEA CUCUMBERS are soft or leathery echinoderms in which the radial pattern is often hard to see. Some are wormlike; some have lost their tubefeet. They live buried in sand or under rocks below the low-tide mark and in deeper water. A ring of short-branched tentacles encircles the mouth. Sea Cucumbers range from 2 to 18 in. long and from ½ to 6 in. thick. Some throw out their internal organs when disturbed and regrow them later. Sea Cucumbers are fairly common on both Atlantic and Pacific shores, usually in cooler water.

4. Northern 9"

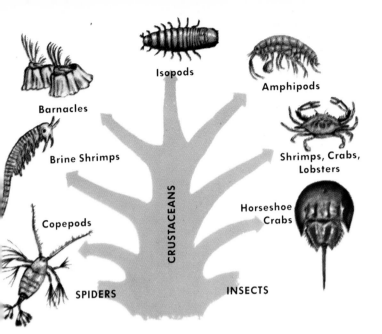

Barnacles

Isopods

Amphipods

Brine Shrimps

Shrimps, Crabs, Lobsters

CRUSTACEANS

Copepods

Horseshoe Crabs

SPIDERS

INSECTS

ARTHROPODS

MARINE ARTHROPODS Almost all of the marine arthropods are crustaceans, a group of some 25,000 species that, though large, pales compared to the roughly 1 million species of insects. Marine crustaceans vary from almost microscopic forms to giants with legs 5 ft. long. Most are small animals. Species of crabs, shrimp, and lobsters are of commercial value. Smaller crustaceans are important foods for many kinds of marine life. All crustaceans have segmented bodies and have an external skeleton. Growth involves shedding the old covering and growing a new one. Less conspicuous arthropods, as the copepods, isopods, and amphipods, are important foods for larger marine life.

ARTHROPODS—over a million species

1,000,000 Insects

20,000 Spiders

25,000 Crustaceans

1,000 Other

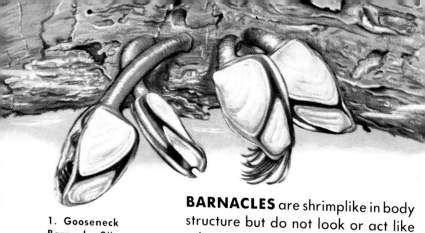

1. Gooseneck Barnacles 2"

2. Rock Barnacles to 2"

BARNACLES are shrimplike in body structure but do not look or act like other crustaceans. Eggs hatch into free-swimming larvae that feed and molt, changing in form as they grow. Soon they attach to rocks or timbers where, after a resting stage, they become shelled adults. The shell is in divisions that overlap and, when shut, are protective. Modified, feathery feet brush plankton and organic matter into the mouth. Some species resist drying and are found well above the low-tide mark. Ship hulls are treated to prevent drag due to barnacle growths.

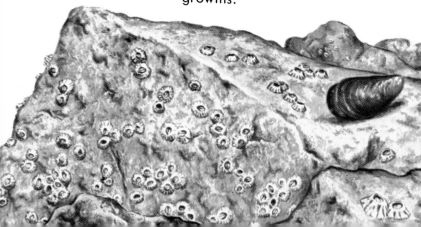

SAND HOPPERS (BEACH FLEAS) and their kin form a group of crustaceans (Amphipods) consisting of more than a thousand species. Most are only a fraction of an inch long. Some live on the dry beaches, in sand and decaying seaweeds. More kinds live in

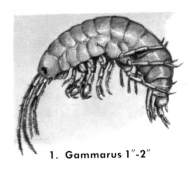

1. Gammarus 1"-2"

sand and mud in shallow water. Others are free-swimming. The name of the group refers to modified legs for both walking and jumping. These thin, laterally compressed animals have gills at the base of appendages for breathing. Some kinds are so numerous during certain seasons that they form a major part of the plankton. The identification of species is difficult for the amateur. Larger, sand-dwelling species are often dug for bait. The plankton species serve as food for many larger kinds of ocean life.

2. Talorchestia 1"

3. California Sand Hopper about 1"

4. Eastern Sand Hopper to 0.5"

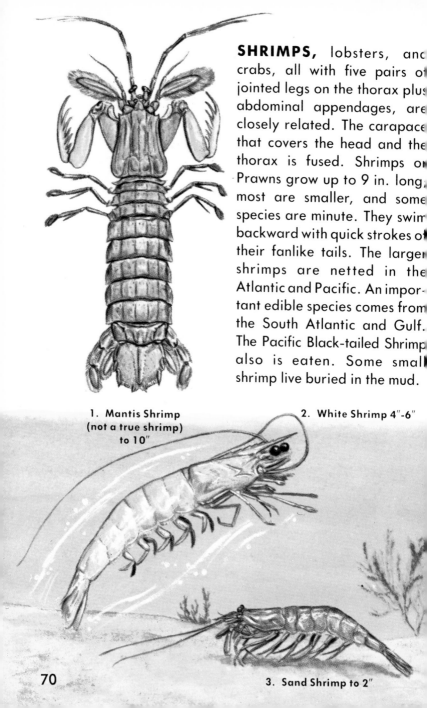

SHRIMPS, lobsters, and crabs, all with five pairs of jointed legs on the thorax plus abdominal appendages, are closely related. The carapace that covers the head and the thorax is fused. Shrimps or Prawns grow up to 9 in. long, most are smaller, and some species are minute. They swim backward with quick strokes of their fanlike tails. The larger shrimps are netted in the Atlantic and Pacific. An important edible species comes from the South Atlantic and Gulf. The Pacific Black-tailed Shrimp also is eaten. Some small shrimp live buried in the mud.

1. Mantis Shrimp
(not a true shrimp)
to 10″

2. White Shrimp 4″-6″

3. Sand Shrimp to 2″

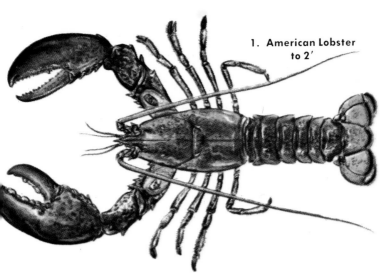

1. **American Lobster to 2'**

LOBSTERS, a seafood favorite, live inshore in summer, in deeper water during the winter. Most caught weigh from 1 to 3 lb.; older lobsters get much larger. It takes about 5 years for them to grow to edible size. Lobsters, captured in wooden traps baited with dead fish, are now protected as the basis of an important industry. The Spiny Lobster of southern waters and of the Pacific is not a close relative. Also edible and more colorful, it lacks the large pincers and has a spiny shell.

2. **Spiny Lobsters 8"-16"**

1. Pacific 1"

2. Atlantic 1.5"

SANDBUGS, sometimes called Mole Crabs, are known to everyone who has waded in the surf. These common crustaceans live in the sand, moving in and out with the tide. Their heavy, curved carapace disguises their relationship to other crabs. Legs are adapted for digging. Plumelike antennae, held just above the sand, catch organic matter on which these active creatures feed. All movements—swimming, crawling, or digging—are made backward. Females, much larger than males, carry their orange eggs several months before they hatch.

digging and feeding

72

Hermit Crab (1"-3") in Moon Shell

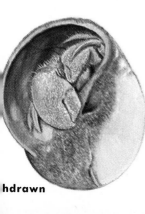

of shell

hdrawn

HERMIT CRABS make up a small but very common group, found in tidal pools and shallow waters all around the world. These interesting crustaceans can be kept alive in salt-water aquaria. An obvious feature of Hermit Crabs is the soft, curved abdomen with a hooklike tail. Smaller Hermit Crabs seek out shells of Peri-winkles and Mudsnails to use as a "house"; larger Hermit Crabs use Whelk, Tulip, and Moon shells. The crabs use only empty shells, searching for bigger ones as they grow. Hermit Crabs are common beach scavengers.

73

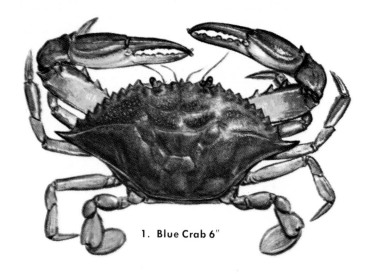

1. Blue Crab 6"

SWIMMING CRABS belong to a family in which the last pair of legs is flattened and adapted for swimming. Best known in this group is the Blue Crab, prized as seafood all along the Atlantic and Gulf coasts, especially in the Chesapeake Bay area. Eggs, laid in summer, remain attached to the body of the female. They hatch in about two weeks into larvae that are very unlike the adults. The young crabs molt and shed their shells as they grow and soon assume adult form. They are mature in about a year. After molting, the shell is soft, and those caught at this time are sold as soft-shelled crabs. They are not a different species as some people may think.

2. Green Crab 3"

Blue Crabs are both predators and scavengers. They prefer brackish water near mouths of rivers, moving into deeper water in winter. Their number may vary considerably from year to year. Other members of the swimming crab group are smaller and have less value, but all are active, attractive animals, alert and aggressive. The Green Crab does not have its legs modified as much for swimming. The Calico or Lady Crab has a varied, speckled pattern, with a shell about as long as it is broad. It prefers sandy beaches and is sometimes caught for food in the South. Portunus Crabs, which are found on both Atlantic and Pacific coasts, include some smaller species that are usually found on seaweeds.

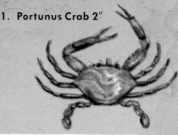

1. Portunus Crab 2"

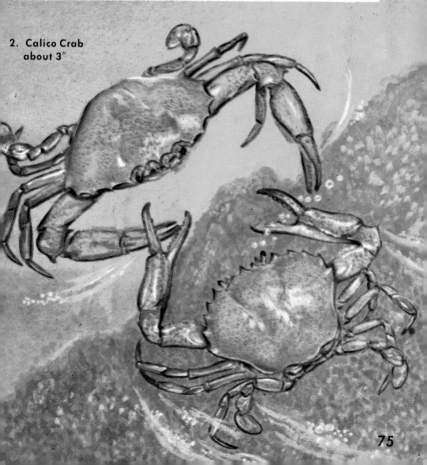

2. Calico Crab about 3"

75

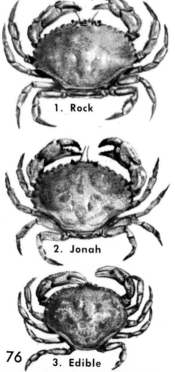

1. Rock

2. Jonah

3. Edible

ROCK CRABS, despite their name, live on sandy bottoms as well as on rocky beaches. On the Pacific Coast, one crab of this group—the Big Crab—grows over a foot across and is caught for market. The crabs prefer cooler waters; they grow larger along the northern shores of both coasts. On the Atlantic Coast are several smaller related species (3 to 4 in.). Young are often found in tidal pools. Larger crabs prefer deeper water. Species differ in markings. All have an oval carapace with teeth along the edge.

1. Fiddler Crabs

FIDDLER and GHOST CRABS are both burrowers, preferring the drier parts of sandy beaches and salt marshes. Both run rapidly with a sidewise motion. The Fiddler Crab is named after the male's huge single claw, which is seldom used except in mating-season battles and territory signalling. These little crabs dig burrows up to 3 ft. long. They feed on organic material in the sand. The Ghost Crab lives in even drier sand than the Fiddler. Its protective coloring and quick movements make it seem to disappear right before your eyes.

2. Ghost Crabs

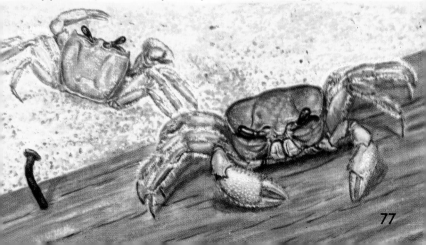

1. Kelp Crab

2. Nine-spined Spider Crab

3. Six-spined Spider Crab

SPIDER and KELP CRABS are closely related. Both have long, thin legs, and a shell more rounded than in swimming crabs. Spider Crabs, which are sluggish, have a carapace usually covered with algae, barnacles, and occasionally a sea anemone. A number of species are found in shallow water on both Atlantic and Pacific shores. The Kelp Crabs of the Pacific have a cleaner carapace than do Spider Crabs. They live in kelp beds and in tidal pools. With their long, agile legs they easily nip an unwary collector.

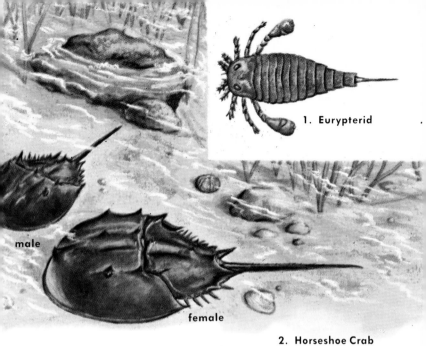

1. Eurypterid

male

female

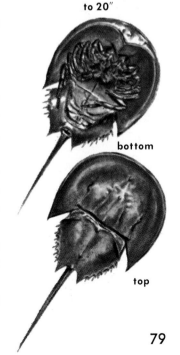

2. Horseshoe Crab
to 20″

bottom

top

HORSESHOE (KING) CRABS

are not crabs but descendants of ancient Eurypterids that flourished some 400 million years ago. These awkward animals are found along Atlantic beaches where they may be very common. None occur along the West Coast. Though bathers are sometimes frightened by them, Horseshoe Crabs are harmless, despite their dangerous-looking spikelike tail. The female is larger than the male. Eggs are deposited in sand close to shore. The young at first look like miniature adults without tails. They live in deeper water, molting periodically as they grow.

79

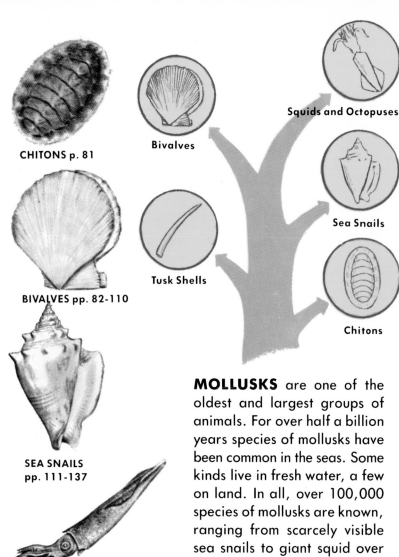

CHITONS p. 81

Bivalves

Squids and Octopuses

Sea Snails

Tusk Shells

BIVALVES pp. 82-110

Chitons

SEA SNAILS
pp. 111-137

SQUIDS and KIN
pp. 138-139

TUSK SHELLS
p. 140

MOLLUSKS are one of the oldest and largest groups of animals. For over half a billion years species of mollusks have been common in the seas. Some kinds live in fresh water, a few on land. In all, over 100,000 species of mollusks are known, ranging from scarcely visible sea snails to giant squid over 50 ft. long. Five classes of mollusks are illustrated at the left. These animals furnish pearls, buttons, ornaments, and food for man, fish, and other sea animals.

80

CHITONS are the most simple mollusks. Their eight over-lapping plates will identify them. The margin of the animal may be smooth, hairy, or spiny. A powerful muscular foot holds chitons to rocks in tidal pools or in shallow water. Most prefer darkness and stay on the underside of the rocks where they feed on diatoms and other small algae. Over a hundred species are found along the Pacific Coast; fewer along the Atlantic, generally in cooler water. A West Coast chiton reaches a length of 12 in., but most are much smaller.

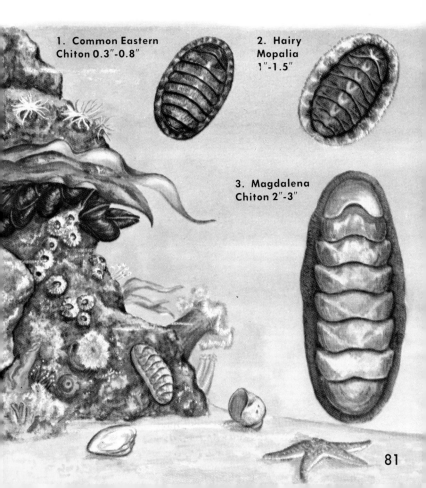

1. **Common Eastern Chiton 0.3"-0.8"**

2. **Hairy Mopalia 1"-1.5"**

3. **Magdalena Chiton 2"-3"**

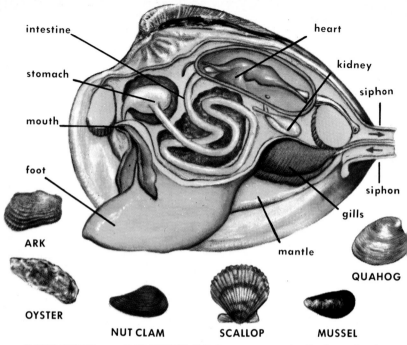

intestine

stomach

mouth

foot

ARK

OYSTER

heart

kidney

siphon

siphon

gills

mantle

QUAHOG

NUT CLAM   SCALLOP   MUSSEL

BIVALVES or PELECYPODS are two-shelled mollusks totaling about 15,000 species, in roughly 70 families. More than 80% are marine, and most of the remaining 20% live in fresh water. The two halves of a bivalve shell are joined at a hinge. One or two powerful muscles hold the valves together, relaxing to allow the siphons to extend. Water enters through one of these paired tubes, bringing oxygen and food to the animal. Water leaves through the other siphon, carrying out waste products.

Bivalves are diverse in form. Some can swim. Some bore in rocks. Most live in sand or mud. These may move by means of a muscular "foot" that is thrust forward and anchored. The animal pulls itself forward as the "foot" is contracted. The animal itself is well developed, with gills for breathing and a heart, liver, kidney, and digestive and reproductive systems. The mantle, a soft membrane around the animal, builds the shells out of lime.

1. Atlantic Nut Clam 0.4"

NUT CLAMS are a large group of small shells. They are actually three related genera—Acila, Nucula, and Nuculana—found on both coasts with a number of widely distributed arctic species. Several are so common that they can be picked up by the handful. A few others are rarely washed ashore. Fishes and diving ducks feed on these bivalves.

2. Divaricate Nut Clam 0.5"

3. Minute Nut Clam 0.5"

5. Pointed Nut Clam 0.3"-0.4"

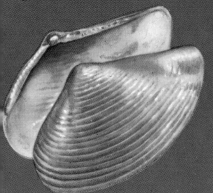

4. Taphria Nut Clam 0.3"-0.8"

hinge line
of Ark Shell

ARK SHELLS are widely distributed, heavy-shelled animals, more common along the Atlantic than on the Pacific. One, the Blood Ark, of shallow sandy bottoms, is the only common mollusk with red blood. Its shell is marked by strong radiating ribs. Another species with prominent ribs is the Eared Ark of southern California shores. Turkey Wing or Zebra Ark, found on the south Atlantic and Gulf shores, is brightly colored when fresh. Ark shells also include a number of miniature species. All Arks have a long, narrow, toothed hinge line.

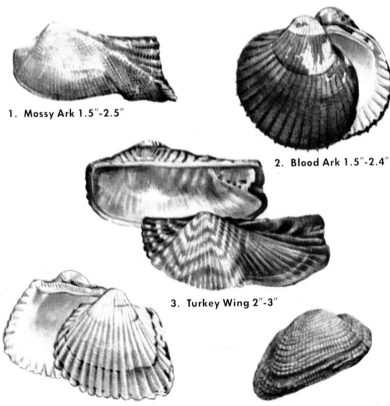

1. Mossy Ark 1.5"-2.5"

2. Blood Ark 1.5"-2.4"

3. Turkey Wing 2"-3"

4. Eared Ark 3"-4"

5. Baily's Miniature Ark 0.3"

Blue Mussels
on piling

1. Blue Mussel 1″-3″

2. Atlantic
Ribbed Mussel 2″-4″

3. Northern
Horse Mussel 2″-6″

MUSSELS, widespread in cooler seas, are a favorite food in Europe, and are gaining in popularity in the United States. Over a dozen species are found in sand or mud or attached to rocks and pilings by strong threads (byssus). The Blue Mussel is very common. The Hooked Mussel, smaller, is found farther south. The Horse Mussel is a deep-water species. Similar kinds are found along the Pacific Coast. These may be poisonous when they feed on certain dinoflagellates.

4. Hooked Mussel 1″

SCALLOPS or PECTENS are common, colorful, and appealing in design. They delight collectors. Rows of tiny eyes along the edge of the mantle make them unique among bivalves. They are jet-propelled. As their valve opens, the space fills with water. The powerful muscle contracts and the valves pull shut, shooting the water out behind and sending the scallop forward. This large muscle is the part most people eat. Most scallops prefer shallow water. Shells are washed up on beaches by storms. Detailed identification involves counting ribs plus noting size, color, and the wings that project at the hinge. Scallops, more common along the Atlantic than Pacific shores, vary in size from 1 to 6 in. or more.

1. Calico Scallop 1"-2"

2. Ornate Scallop 1"-1.3'

3. Giant Rock Scallop 8"

1. Pacific Pink Scallop 2"-2.8"

2. Kelp-weed Scallop 1"

3. Sentis Scallop 1"-1.5"

4. Atlantic Deep-sea Scallop 5"-8"

5. San Diego Scallop 3"

6. Atlantic Bay Scallop 2"

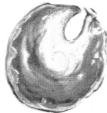

1. Atlantic Jingle Shell 1"-2"

2. **Prickly Jingle Shell**
to 0.8"

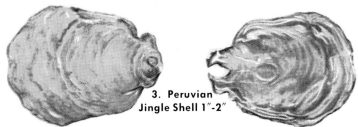

3. **Peruvian**
Jingle Shell 1"-2"

JINGLE SHELLS, thin, bright, and pearly, are very common on both coasts, mainly in warmer waters. The shells, about 1 in. across, are unequal, the top one being deeply hollowed, the bottom one smaller and almost flat. The animal anchors itself permanently to rocks, seaweeds, or old shells by a fleshy appendage (byssus) passing through a hole in the lower valve. Only the upper valve is usually washed ashore.

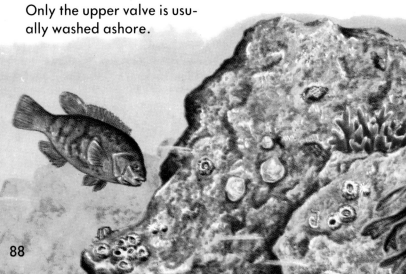

OYSTERS, the most valuable shell-fish, are common in shallow, warmer waters of all oceans. The shells are irregular in shape; the valves, un-equal in size. When young, oysters are free-swimming; later they attach themselves to shells, rocks, or roots. Most species of oysters are too small to be used as food, though they are eaten by land and other marine animals.

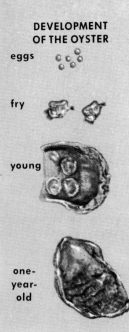

DEVELOPMENT
OF THE OYSTER

eggs

fry

young

one-
year-
old

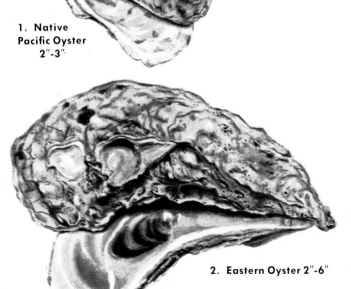

1. Native
Pacific Oyster
2"-3"

2. Eastern Oyster 2"-6"

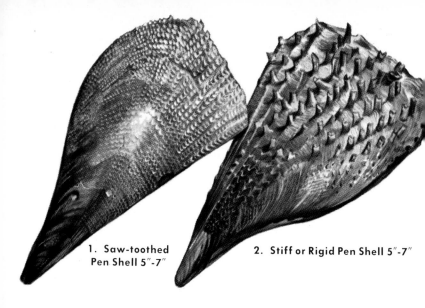

1. Saw-toothed
   Pen Shell 5″-7″

2. Stiff or Rigid Pen Shell 5″-7″

PEN SHELLS or SEA PENS are large, wedge-shaped shells. The animals grow 4 in. to almost 1 ft. long. Their large muscle, like that of a scallop, is sometimes used for food. Pen Shells prefer warmer water where they bury themselves in mud or sand and attach themselves to a rock or some other solid object. They are quite rare on the Pacific· Coast, though three species are common in the Atlantic. The shells are thin and fragile, dull-colored and rough. The insides are smooth and pearly.

3. Amber Pen Shell 4″-7″

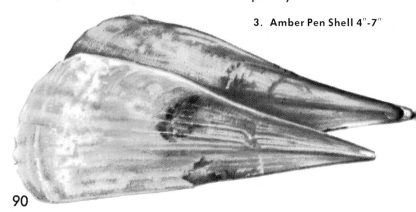

1. Atlantic Wing Oyster 1.5"-5"

WING and PEARL OYS-TERS are widespread in warmer waters. The Great Pearl Oyster, source of most pearl and mother-of-pearl, is a large (12 in.) tropical animal. Pearls are found in shells over 5 years old. Often the pearls are too small to have value, or if the pearls are attached to the shell, they are worthless as gems. Cultured pearls are produced by placing balls of shell under the mantle of Pearl Oysters.

2. Atlantic Pearl Oyster
1.5"-3"

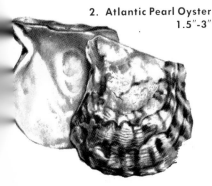

2. Say's Pandora 0.8"-1"

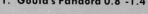

1. Gould's Pandora 0.8"-1.4"

4. Western Pandora 1"

3. Punctate Pandora 2"

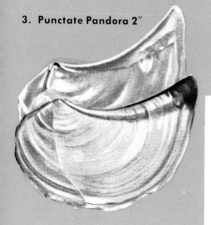

PANDORA SHELLS include over six common species found on both the Atlantic and Pacific coasts. They may occur below the low-tide mark or are dredged up from moderately shallow waters. Pandoras are small shells, rarely over 1½ in. long, usually shorter. The shells are thin, with unequal flattened valves. The right valve is much more flattened than the left. Their color is white, sometimes chalky, and a pearly under-layer may be revealed when the shell is worn. A strong ridge along the hinge line is characteristic. The hinge is toothed. Gould's Pandora, often found from North Carolina northward to Labrador, has a pair of purplish fringed siphons. The Lyonsias and Thracias are related groups, the former somewhat smaller and the latter usually larger than Pandoras. Conrad's Thracia (3 to 4 in.) has a rounded shell with the ridge along the hinge line not strongly developed.

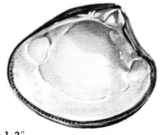

1. **Waved Astarte** 1.3"

2. **Smooth or Chestnut Astarte** 1"

3. **Striate or Boreal Astarte** 0.5"

4. **Alaska Astarte** 1"

5. **Esquimalt Astarte** 0.5"

ASTARTES, also known as Chestnut Clams, are commonly washed up on beaches. The animals live in shallow or moderately deep water. Their tissues are of a red or orange color. Astartes are small (from ½ to 2 in.), roughly triangular, and have a heavy shell. The concentric grooves and ridges are strong in some species. These animals live in cooler waters, north to the Arctic, but two kinds occur as far south as Florida.

1. Florida Lucina 1.5"

2. Western Ringed Lucina 2"-2.5"

3. Tiger Lucina 2.5"-3.5"

4. Pennsylvania Lucina 1"-2"

LUCINA or WHITE SHELLS are members of a tropical family common in warmer waters along both Atlantic and Pacific shores. They live on sandy or muddy bottoms in shallow water or moderate depths. Shells are rough, ½ to 3½ in. across, usually white. The surface may be ridged, and some species have a deep fold running from the tip of the shell to the margin. Eggs are sometimes retained within the gill chamber while they develop.

COCKLE or HEART SHELLS are close relatives of the edible European Cockle. All the shells are heart-shaped, with strong radiating ribs. Valves are of equal size. The animals live in sand and mud. They prefer shallow water, often in brackish inlets. They are active and may jump several inches using their powerful foot. The Iceland Cockle is found in cooler waters of both oceans. Yellow Cockle, yellowish with brown, has 30 to 40 ribs. It occurs south from the Carolinas. Nuttall's Cockle is an abundant Pacific species; white or yellow with strong squarish ribs. The Giant Atlantic Cockle has 30 to 36 ribs, and the margins of its valves are toothed. It is common along the south Atlantic and Gulf coasts.

1. Iceland Cockle 2.5"

2. Yellow Cockle 2"

3. Nuttall's Cockle 3"-6"

4. Giant
Atlantic Cockle 3"-5"

1. Southern Quahog

QUAHOGS or HARD-SHELL CLAMS are a small but important group of bivalves. Related tropical forms are beautifully shaped and marked. The typical Atlantic Coast species (3 to 5 in.), called Quahog by the Indians and also Littleneck or Cherrystone Clams (for small sizes), is less attractive but more appetizing. It was used as food by the Indians and has been eaten ever since, fresh and in chowders. The Southern Quahog is larger, with a heavier shell. Both are found in sand or mud near the low-tide mark. The coastal Indians made wampum from the white and purple

2. Northern Quahog with foot and siphons extended

Northern Quahog

parts of the Quahog shell. Purple wampum was highly prized. The shells were broken, drilled, and rubbed down to make beads about ¼ in. long. These were strung in short strands or woven into belts. Wampum belts served to bind treaties; shorter strings were used in trade.

wampum beads (enlarged)

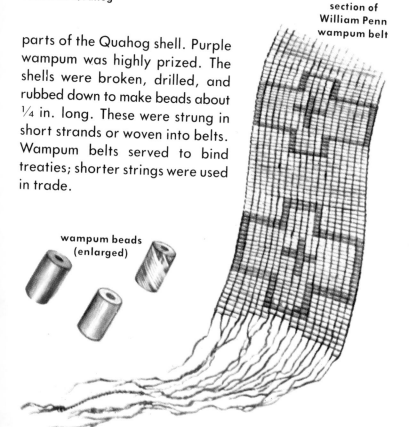

1. Thin-shelled Littleneck about 4"

ROCK VENUS SHELLS or LITTLENECKS are Pacific species that include the most common clams of the Pacific Coast. Common Pacific Littleneck is the hardshell clam of sandy bottoms, most common north of San Francisco. It occurs in several forms or varieties. One of these, the Rough-sided Littleneck, more common to the south, is marked by prominent lines on the shell. The Thin-shelled Littleneck is a large species, relatively flatter, with fewer markings and light grayish brown in color.

2. Common Pacific Littleneck 1.5"-2"—two forms

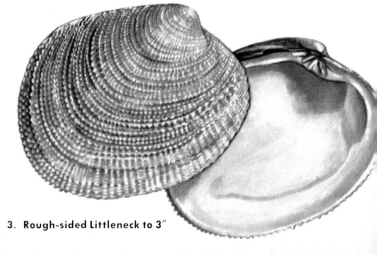

3. Rough-sided Littleneck to 3"

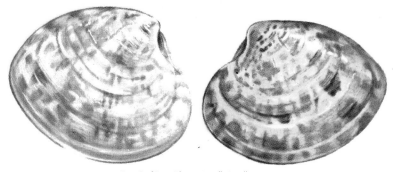

1. Calico Clam 1.5"-2.5"

CALICO CLAMS are attractive mollusks of the southern Atlantic and Gulf coasts. The elongate Sunray Venus or Sunray Shell, best known in this group, is pink, gray, and lavender. Interior is pink. The animal lives in sand just below the tide mark. The smaller, more robust Calico Clam is known also as the Checkerboard, from the square, brownish spots on the thick, smooth valves. The interior is white. This species occurs south of the Carolinas and is especially common along the shores of Florida's west coast.

2. Sunray Venus 4"-5"

1. Elegant Dosinia 2"-3"

2. Disc Dosinia 2"-3"

AMETHYST GEM CLAM and DOSINIAS are Atlantic
Coast shells. The Amethyst Gem Clam is a small, pea-
sized, smooth shell found commonly all along the Atlantic

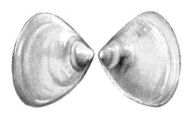

3. Amethyst Gem Clam 0.3"

Coast and to as far north as
Nova Scotia. Exterior, lavender to purple; interior, paler.
This small clam has been introduced with oysters into Puget
Sound. Closely related are two
species of Dosinia. Both have
thin, shiny, white, circular
shells. The more common kind
has a fine, yellowish skin over
the white shell. Dosinias live in
sand in shallow southern
waters.

PISMO CLAMS, famous for their flavor, are found on open, sandy beaches from mid-California south. Commercial digging has so reduced the number of Pismo Clams that the law permits a person to dig only a few clams daily (check current law before digging). Even so, there is danger of their disappearing from California beaches. The thick, smooth, gray to brown shells are almost triangular. Pismo Clams take 4 to 7 years to grow 5 in. (present legal minimum for digging), but they may continue to grow more slowly for another 10 years.

1. Bodega Tellin
to 2"

2. Carpenter's Tellin 0.4"

3. Sunrise Tellin 2"-4"

4. Salmon Tellin 0.5"

5. Modest Tellin 0.8"-1"

6. Speckled Tellin 2.5"-3.5"

7. Rose Petal Tellin 1.5"

TELLIN SHELLS belong to a family which is often considered the aristocracy of the bivalves. Of several hundred species, a score and more are found along our coasts, especially in the warmer waters of the Atlantic and Gulf. Tellin Shells are diverse in size (¼ to 4 in.), but all are relatively thin and compressed. The hinge is not strong, and shells washed up on the beach are often broken apart.

The delicately colored shells are white, yellow, pink, and purple, varying with the individuals and species. On the Pacific Coast look for the Modest, Salmon, and Carpenter's Tellins. The South Atlantic Coast has a greater variety and includes such well-known kinds as the Sunrise Tellin, Dwarf Tellin, Tampa Tellin, and Rose Petal Tellin.

1. **Tenta Macoma** 0.5"-0.8"

2. **Balthic Macoma** 0.5"-1.5"

3. **Constricted Macoma** 1"-2.5"

4. **White Sand Macoma** 2"-4"

MACOMA SHELLS are another widespread group, larger than the Tellins and not as attractive. These thin, glossy shells are usually white but are sometimes covered with a thin, brownish membrane. While some species live in cooler water, others extend far into the tropics. They tend to favor muddy bottoms in protected waters.

5. **Indented Macoma** 1.5"

6. **Bent-nose Macoma** 2"-3.5" 103

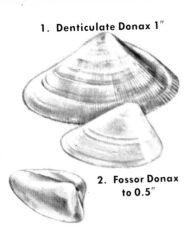

1. Denticulate Donax 1"

2. Fossor Donax to 0.5"

3. California Donax to 1"

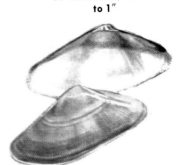

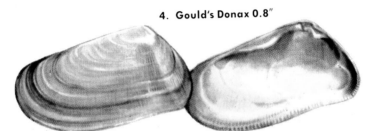

4. Gould's Donax 0.8"

COQUINA, DONAX, or WEDGE SHELLS live in sand close to shore in warm waters of the Atlantic, Pacific, and Gulf. Some kinds are so abundant that, despite their small size, they are dug to make chowder. Along the South Atlantic the Coquina is also called Pompano Shell and Butterfly Shell. The last name refers to the fact that valves, washed ashore, often remain attached but spread open like butterfly wings. All Donax shells show great variation in color and markings. A handful picked up at random will illustrate this.

5. Coquina 0.5"-0.8"

1. Rosy Razor 1″-3″

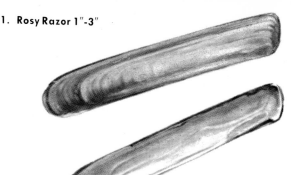

2. Atlantic Razor to 10″

3. Green Razor 2″

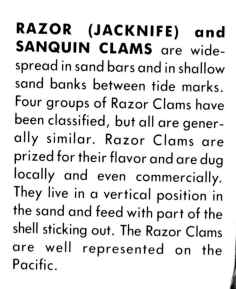

RAZOR (JACKNIFE) and SANQUIN CLAMS are widespread in sand bars and in shallow sand banks between tide marks. Four groups of Razor Clams have been classified, but all are generally similar. Razor Clams are prized for their flavor and are dug locally and even commercially. They live in a vertical position in the sand and feed with part of the shell sticking out. The Razor Clams are well represented on the Pacific.

4. Stout Tagelus 2″-3.5″

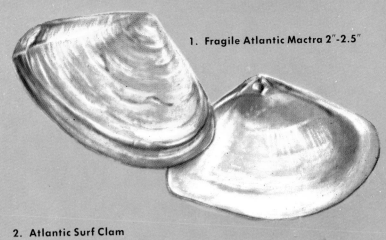

1. Fragile Atlantic Mactra 2"-2.5"

2. Atlantic Surf Clam to 7"

SURF CLAMS include several related groups, all of them preferring a surf environment on sandy shores. These clams burrow a few inches into the sand, feeding on tiny plankton organisms which are washed back and forth by the waves.

The Atlantic Surf Clam has a coarse white shell. It is often gathered for food. After severe storms, beaches are

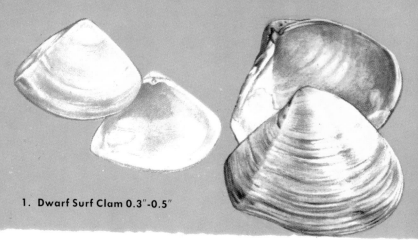

1. Dwarf Surf Clam 0.3"-0.5"

2. Smooth Duck Clam 2"-3"

sometimes covered with millions of these clams. The Dwarf Surf Clam is very common in warm, shallow waters of the Atlantic and Gulf, favoring the protected waters of sounds and estuaries rather than the surf. The Fragile Atlantic Mactra and California Mactra are species with both ends of the shell rounded. Only the eastern form has a fragile shell. Duck Clams are similar eastern clams with thin shells. They show a greater preference for mud than do the thin-shelled Fragile Atlantic Mactras.

3. Channeled Duck Clam 2"-3"

SOFT-SHELL CLAMS prefer shallow, muddy bottoms. At low tide, clam diggers locate them as they squirt. Known also as Steamer Clams and Long Clams, they are edible, tasty, and popular. The shell is dull chalky white, with unequal valves that do not close completely. Soft-shell clams are abundant along the Atlantic Coast, and they have been introduced into the San Francisco Bay region.

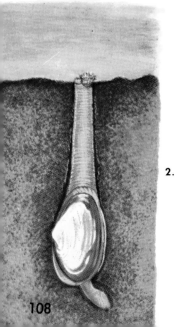

1. **Truncate Soft-shell Clam 1"-3"**

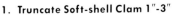

2. **Soft-shell Clam 1"-6"**

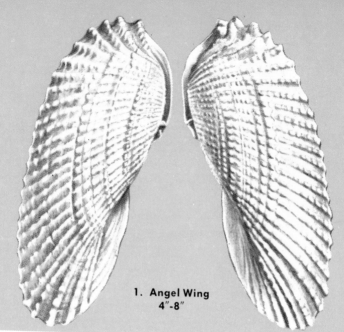

1. Angel Wing
4"–8"

ANGEL WINGS and similar bivalves are species that burrow in mud, clay, or peat and cannot be collected without hard, careful digging. The Angel Wing lives about a foot below the surface. These species live along the Atlantic, generally preferring warmer water. A number of similar but less attractive species live along the Pacific. Shells of all are thin, somewhat fragile, and often pinkish.

2. False Angel Wing 2"

3. Fallen Angel Wing 2"–2.5"

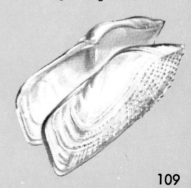

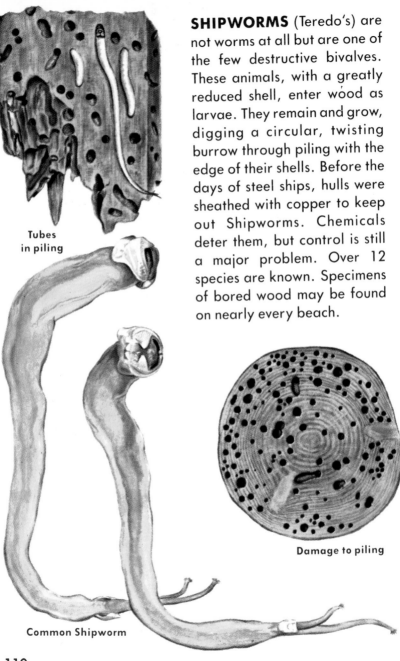

SHIPWORMS (Teredo's) are not worms at all but are one of the few destructive bivalves. These animals, with a greatly reduced shell, enter wood as larvae. They remain and grow, digging a circular, twisting burrow through piling with the edge of their shells. Before the days of steel ships, hulls were sheathed with copper to keep out Shipworms. Chemicals deter them, but control is still a major problem. Over 12 species are known. Specimens of bored wood may be found on nearly every beach.

Tubes in piling

Damage to piling

Common Shipworm

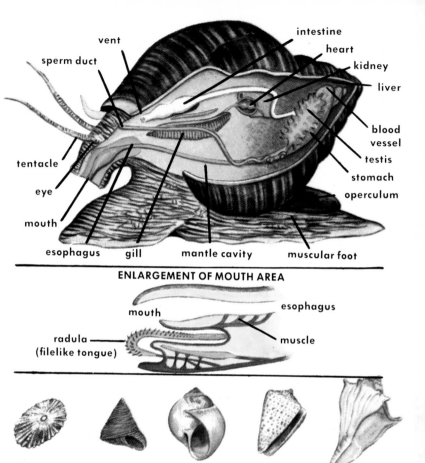

ENLARGEMENT OF MOUTH AREA

LIMPET   TOP SHELL   MOON SHELL   CONE SHELL   WHELK

UNIVALVES or GASTROPODS, often called Sea Snails, are the second largest group of mollusks. It includes many fresh-water and land species; the latter are most common in the tropics. Though a few have no shell at all, most have a single spiral shell. The animal has a distinct head with eyes and feelers (tentacles). Internal body structures shown above are modified to fit the spiral pattern, evident even in the young, free-swimming larvae. A horny cover or operculum covers the shell opening and protects the animal when it withdraws.

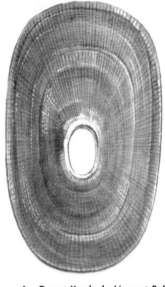

1. Great Keyhole Limpet 2.5"-6"

2. Rough Limpet 1.3"

3. Antillean Limpet 0.8"-1"

4. Lister's Keyhole Limpet 1"-2"

LIMPETS have spiral shells as larvae but soon settle down and grow their flattened conical shells. A number of species have a hole at the peak of the spiral; others do not. Most prefer cooler waters of the Atlantic and Pacific. Most grow attached to rocks and may be collected at low tides. Some prefer deeper water, and a few live on larger algae.

The Great Keyhole Limpet of the Pacific is our largest species. Its black mantle covers most of shell.

5. Atlantic Plate Limpet 1"-1.5"

1. Chestnut Turban 1"-1.5"

operculum

TOP SHELLS and those on the next page point out the wide confusion in common names. Over 50 American species are called Top Shells, including those illustrated. Some have a thick, heavy operculum that covers the animal when inside the shell. Larger species are gathered for food, especially on the Asian side of the Pacific. Found mainly in cool, shallow to moderately deep water, most species cling to rocks.

2. Ribbed Top Shell 0.8"-1"

3. Greenland Margarite 0.5"

4. Tampa or Jujube Top Shell 0.5"-1.3"

5. Channeled Top Shell 1"-1.5"

1. Black Tegula 1"-1.5"
(3 views)

TEGULA SHELLS, sometimes called Turban Shells because of their shape, are algae-eating snails of warmer waters. Nearly a dozen species live along the Pacific, but only two occur in shallow waters of southern Florida. West Indies species are more common. All have smooth, iridescent shells; there is a thin, horny, sheet-like covering on the shells of living animals. The Black Tegula is abundant on Pacific shores between the tide marks. The top of the shell is usually worn, disclosing the pearly layer beneath the dark skin. The Speckled Tegula is also a Pacific species, its color more grayish.

2. Speckled Tegula 1"-1.5"

3. Smooth Atlantic Tegula 0.5"-0.8" (2 views)

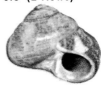

1. Red Abalone 10"-12"

2. Pinto Abalone 4"-6"

live Red Abalone

3. Green Abalone 7"-8"

ABALONES, largest and most attractive Pacific Coast shells, are most common in warm waters. The flat shells, iridescent on the inside, were prized by Indians and traded far inland. They are still used in attractive jewelry. The large muscle is edible and tasty. Abalones are sold fresh in markets and are featured in restaurants. Many are canned for shipping. Harvesting is controlled by laws.

4. Black Abalone 6"

1. Brown-banded Wentletrap 0.5"-1"

2. Greenland Wentletrap 1"

WENTLETRAPS are Staircase or Ladder Shells. The first name, Wentletrap, is Dutch; it is applied to old spiral staircases. Delicate, symmetrical, and attractive—rare forms of these shells bring high prices from collectors. The animals are carnivorous. Wentletraps live in shallow to deep waters, some species at depths of more than half a mile. They are an important food of larger fish. The shell is a tight whorl with as many as ten spirals. The lip of the shell thickens, forming an isolated ridge during the next growth period.

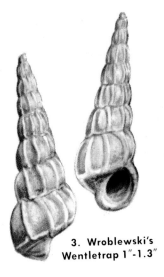

3. Wroblewski's Wentletrap 1"-1.3"

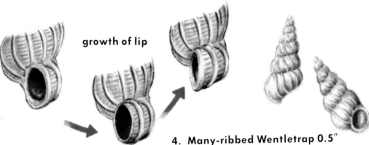

growth of lip

4. Many-ribbed Wentletrap 0.5"

MOON SHELLS and the closely related Natica include about a dozen widely distributed species. Their shells are found on all Atlantic and Pacific beaches. These carnivores feed on other shellfish, which they hold down with their unusually large foot and then drill a hole through the shell with their toothy tongue, or radula. Moon Shells build a circular "sand collar," cementing the sand grains with a glue they produce. Eggs are deposited inside this protective ring.

1. **Arctic Natica 1"-1.3"**

2. **Colorful Atlantic Natica 1"-2"**

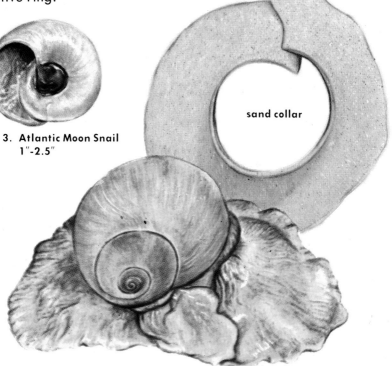

3. **Atlantic Moon Snail 1"-2.5"**

sand collar

4. **Common Northern Moon Shell 2"-4.5"**

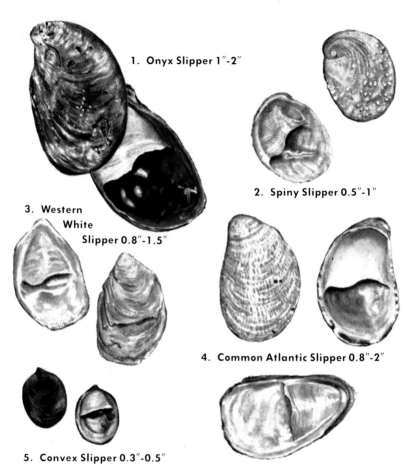

1. Onyx Slipper 1"-2"

2. Spiny Slipper 0.5"-1"

3. Western White Slipper 0.8"-1.5"

4. Common Atlantic Slipper 0.8"-2"

5. Convex Slipper 0.3"-0.5"

6. Eastern White Slipper 0.5"-1.5"

BOAT SHELLS or SLIPPERS lead a fixed existence somewhat like that of Limpets. Inside each shell is a small horizontal platform or deck resembling that on an old sailing ship. This and the shape of the shell give these species their name. Collectors find these common shells washed up on every beach. The animals live in shallow water attached to rocks or other shells. Slippers occur in all the temperate and tropical seas. There are about nine American species.

PERIWINKLES are probably better known than any other mollusks. The common species has come from Europe, where it is a favored food. During the past century it has spread rapidly along the Atlantic Coast, but it is seldom eaten in the United States. About 12 species are equally distributed on rocky beaches of both our coasts. All are drab-colored, though some are spotted or mottled. Periwinkles feed on algae scraped from rocks or other surfaces with their tongues.

1. Checkered
Periwinkle 0.5″

2. Eroded
Periwinkle
0.5″-0.8″

3. Northern Rough
Periwinkle 0.3″-0.5″

4. Marsh
Periwinkle 1″

Common Periwinkles
on seaweed

5. Common European Periwinkle
0.8″-1″

6. Angulate Periwinkle 1″

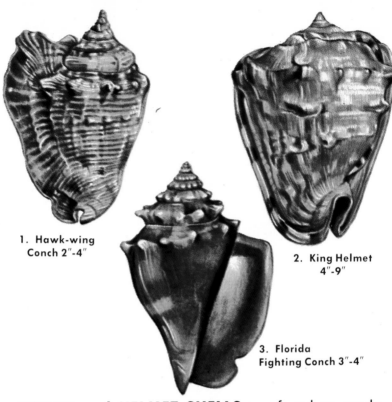

1. Hawk-wing
Conch 2"-4"

2. King Helmet
4"-9"

3. Florida
Fighting Conch 3"-4"

CONCH and HELMET SHELLS are found on sandy bottoms of shallow tropical waters. Species of these widespread groups occur from the Carolinas south. Shells are often for sale in stores and roadside stands. All are large. Helmet Shells are carnivorous. Conchs feed on algae. The Queen Conch, one of the largest univalves or gastropods, is commonly eaten in the form of chowder. The heavy, triangular, thick-lipped Helmet Shells are used in making cameos. The thick shell and variable colors suit them especially well for this purpose.

living Queen Conch

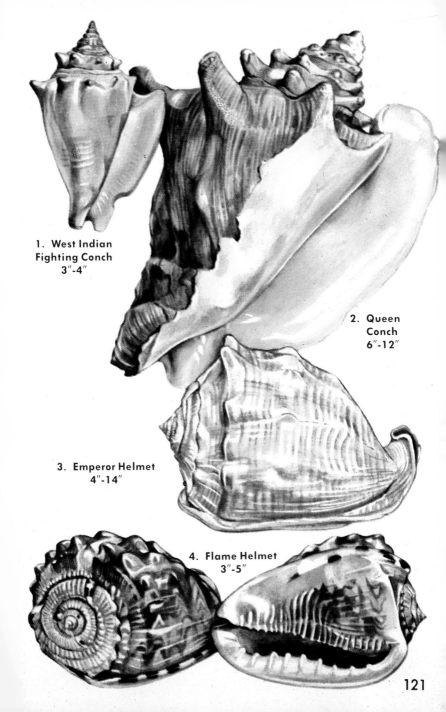

1. West Indian
Fighting Conch
3"-4"

2. Queen
Conch
6"-12"

3. Emperor Helmet
4"-14"

4. Flame Helmet
3"-5"

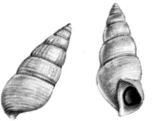

1. Alternate Bittium 0.2"-0.3"

HORNSHELLS and CER-ITHS are small animals that live on mud and seaweeds and in tidal pools along both coasts. They are common on such sea plants as eelgrass, where they feed on detritus and microscopic organisms. Most prefer shallow water and so are most abundant in the tidal zone. Atlantic species are more common on Florida and other southern beaches. Some Pacific species prefer colder water. All these animals have sharply spired shells with from 10 to 15 or more spirals. About 100 species totally.

2. California Hornshell 1"-1.3"

3. False Cerith 0.5"-0.8"

4. Florida Cerith 1"-1.5"

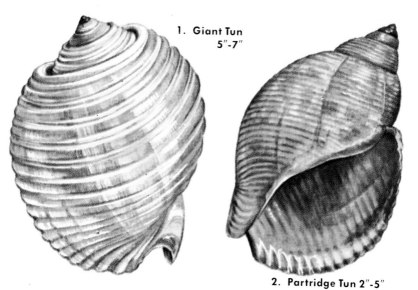

1. **Giant Tun**
   5"-7"

2. **Partridge Tun** 2"-5"

TUN or CASK SHELLS are large, thin-walled, rounded shells, mostly tropical. A few species occur on our southern Atlantic Coast—none off California. The moving animal is much larger and, like some other gastropods, seems too big for its shell. Members of this family prefer deeper water. Fig Shell, shown here with the live animal protruding from its shell, is a close relative. Both Tun and Fig Shells are carnivorous.

3. **Common Fig Shell** 3"-4"

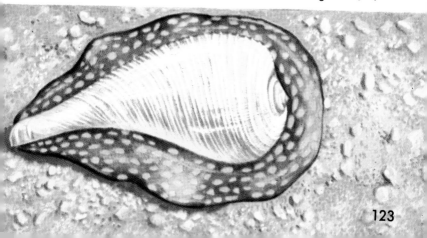

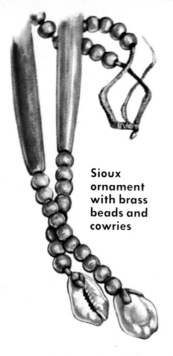

Sioux ornament with brass beads and cowries

COWRIES have attracted people the world over by their beauty. The smooth colorful shells of smaller kinds have been made into ornaments, and a yellow species was long traded and used as money in Africa and other regions. The spiral shell of cowries can be seen only in young animals. As the animal grows, the lime deposited in the large body spiral gradually engulfs the remaining twists of the shell. In mature cowries, all trace of the spiral shell is lost. All cowries have highly polished shells; a few are plain, but many are mottled and brightly colored. All are tropical species, and only a limited number occur in our warmer waters—one on the Pacific Coast and about a dozen on the Atlantic. Most prefer moderately deep water.

The Coffee Bean Shells, or Trivias, are smaller relatives of cowries, and are all less than 1 in. long. A closely related group is found along the Pacific.

live Chestnut Cowry

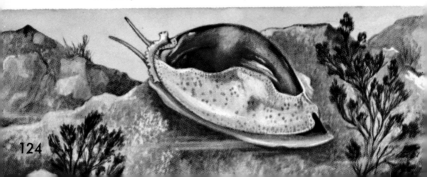

2. Atlantic Yellow Cowry
0.5″-1.3″

3. Atlantic
Gray Cowry
0.8″-1.5″

1. Chestnut Cowry
1″-2″

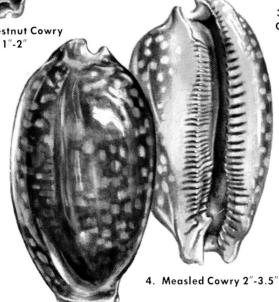

4. Measled Cowry 2″-3.5″

5. Solander's Coffee
Bean 0.8″

6. California
Coffee Bean 0.3″-0.5″

7. Four-spotted
Coffee Bean
0.1″-0.3″

8. Atlantic
Coffee
Bean 0.5″

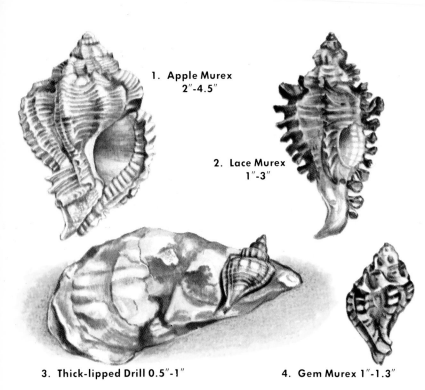

1. Apple Murex
2"-4.5"

2. Lace Murex
1"-3"

3. Thick-lipped Drill 0.5"-1"

4. Gem Murex 1"-1.3"

MUREX SHELLS and their kin include over a thousand species, counting the Drills (p. 128) that have become serious pests in oyster beds. All of this group are carnivores, feeding mainly on bivalves. Their shells are heavy, ridged, and usually spiny. Most showy species are tropical, though some are also found in temperate waters. Typical and best known is the Murex group, a widespread genus, found on our southern Atlantic and Gulf coasts, and farther south. The large, showy West Indian Murex is a rare species. Fewer kinds, and a number of related species, live on our Pacific shores. Murex snails live in moderately deep water. Shells are often washed up on beaches. The Drills and other shallow-water species can be collected at low tides.

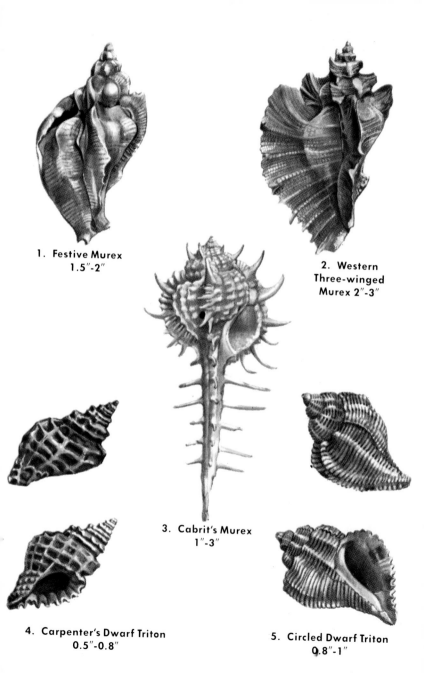

1. Festive Murex
1.5"-2"

2. Western
Three-winged
Murex 2"-3"

3. Cabrit's Murex
1"-3"

4. Carpenter's Dwarf Triton
0.5"-0.8"

5. Circled Dwarf Triton
0.8"-1"

127

OYSTER DRILLS, DOGWINKLES, and PURPURAS

look like miniature, less showy forms of Murex shells. Oyster Drills use their radula (filelike tongue) to drill a hole through bivalve shells and then suck out the soft animal inside. Animals of this group (and some species of Murex, too) were crushed to obtain the famous royal purple dye used by Greeks and Romans. These animals are common on rocks and in tidal pools on both our coasts and in shallow temperate waters around the world.

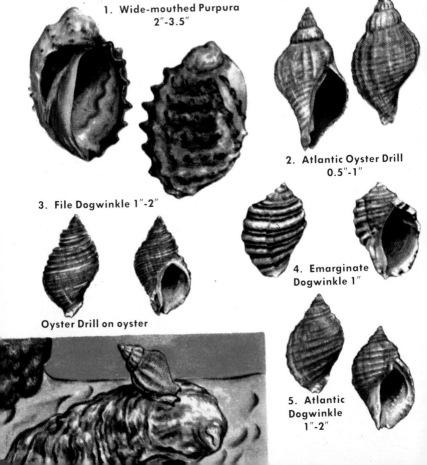

1. Wide-mouthed Purpura
2"-3.5"

2. Atlantic Oyster Drill
0.5"-1"

3. File Dogwinkle 1"-2"

4. Emarginate Dogwinkle 1"

Oyster Drill on oyster

5. Atlantic Dogwinkle 1"-2"

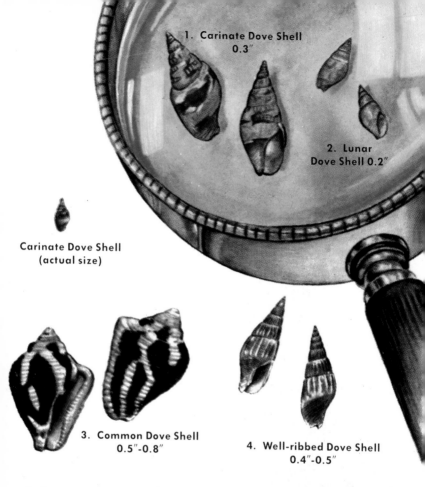

1. **Carinate Dove Shell**
0.3"

2. **Lunar Dove Shell** 0.2"

Carinate Dove Shell
(actual size)

3. **Common Dove Shell**
0.5"-0.8"

4. **Well-ribbed Dove Shell**
0.4"-0.5"

DOVE SHELLS would be an even more attractive group of shells if only they were larger. All of the American species are well under an inch long. These small animals are common and can be collected as they crawl over rocks and seaweeds at low tide. The spindle-shaped shells have a thickening at the center of the lip. They are shiny and often brightly marked. Dove Shells occur along the full length of each coast but they are more common in warmer waters and with more species along the East Coast than along the West.

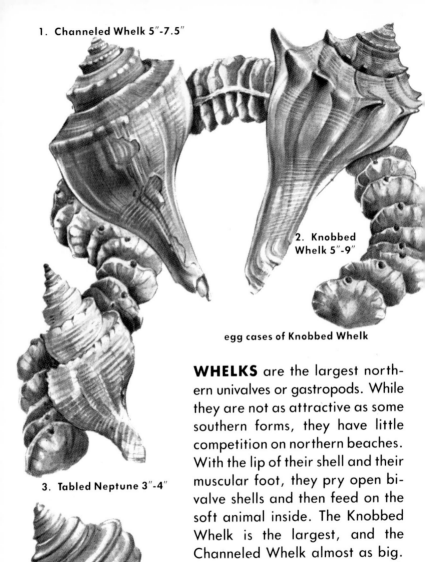

1. Channeled Whelk 5″-7.5″

2. Knobbed Whelk 5″-9″

egg cases of Knobbed Whelk

3. Tabled Neptune 3″-4″

4. New England Neptune 3″-4.5″

WHELKS are the largest northern univalves or gastropods. While they are not as attractive as some southern forms, they have little competition on northern beaches. With the lip of their shell and their muscular foot, they pry open bivalve shells and then feed on the soft animal inside. The Knobbed Whelk is the largest, and the Channeled Whelk almost as big. Both occur from Cape Cod south along Atlantic and Gulf shores. In summer, strings of horny egg cases of these whelks are found on the beach—sometimes with hundreds of very tiny perfect shells within. The

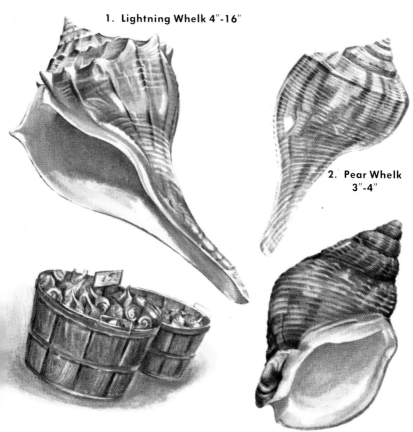

1. **Lightning Whelk 4″-16″**

2. **Pear Whelk 3″-4″**

3. **Common Northern Buccinum 2″-4″**

Pear Whelk, more delicately formed, is a southern whelk. Dozens of smaller whelks also occur along northern shores. All are carnivores and scavengers. Some are widely used as food in Europe. The Knobbed and Channeled Whelks also are eaten and are sometimes found in markets.

4. **Glacial Whelk 2″-3″**

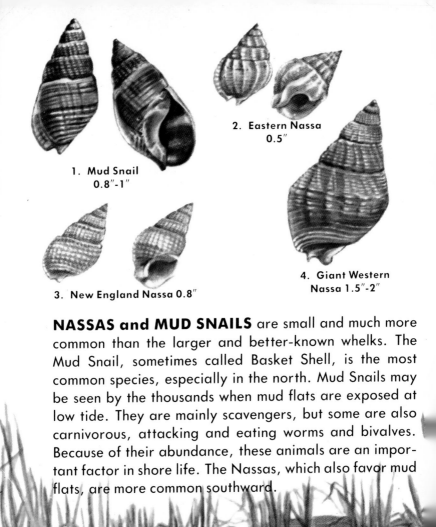

1. Mud Snail
0.8"-1"

2. Eastern Nassa
0.5"

3. New England Nassa 0.8"

4. Giant Western
Nassa 1.5"-2"

NASSAS and MUD SNAILS are small and much more common than the larger and better-known whelks. The Mud Snail, sometimes called Basket Shell, is the most common species, especially in the north. Mud Snails may be seen by the thousands when mud flats are exposed at low tide. They are mainly scavengers, but some are also carnivorous, attacking and eating worms and bivalves. Because of their abundance, these animals are an important factor in shore life. The Nassas, which also favor mud flats, are more common southward.

1. Banded Tulip
2"-4"

TULIP or BAND SHELLS are large, thick-shelled univalves, or gastropods, of warmer seas. They feed on other mollusks. Three species live on our south Atlantic shores. Some smaller related shells, belonging to the same family, are found along the California beaches. Best known of this group is the Florida Horse Conch, the largest in American waters. The living animal is even more attractive than its handsomely colored shell.

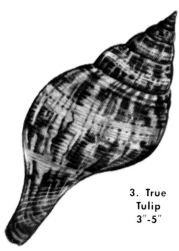

2. Florida
Horse Conch
1'-2'

3. True
Tulip
3"-5"

133

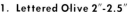

1. Lettered Olive 2″-2.5″

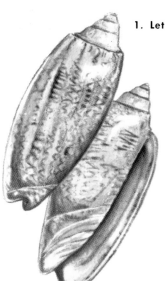

2. Variable Dwarf Olive 0.3″-0.5″

3. Beatic Dwarf Olive 0.5″-0.8″

**4. Purple Dwarf Olive
1″-1.3″**

OLIVE SHELLS are small and somewhat similar to Cowries (pp. 124-125) in that the growing shell engulfs much of its spire. The family is a large one of many tropical species. Our species occur on both the Atlantic and Pacific coasts—some extending into northern waters. The animal is quite large, and when it is completely extended, the shell is hidden. The shiny, bright gray or bluish shells were prized ornaments of Indians. Olive Shells are common in shallow water and are found on sandy beaches.

1. California Cone 0.8"-1"

CONE SHELLS are a tropical group. This large family is represented by a single species on our Pacific shores and by about a dozen Atlantic species, mainly from Florida's rocks and corals. More common in the West Indies. Some tropical species are poisonous and can give a fatal "sting" with poison injected through their harpoonlike tongue. But none of these lives in our area. Cone Shells are brightly colored in yellows and browns and are best identified by their typical conical shape and attractive markings. They are favorites of collectors and the rare Glory-of-the-Seas from the East Indies is the most valuable of all shells.

2. Mouse Cone 1"-1.5"

4. Florida Cone 1.5"-1.8"

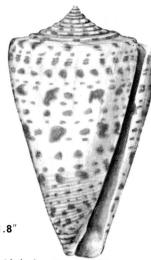

3. Crown Cone 2"-3"

5. Alphabet Cone 2"-3"

135

1. California Bubble
1.5"-2"

2. Eastern Paper or Glassy Bubb
0.5"

4. West Indian Bubble
0.5"-1"

**3. Brown-lined
Paper Bubble 1"-1.5"**

**5. Striate
Bubble 0.8"-1"**

BUBBLE SHELLS belong to several closely related families that differ from other univalves, or gastropods, in several ways. The animal has two pairs of tentacles. The shell is smaller than the animal, loosely curved, thin and brittle. Most species are carnivorous, and they live in shallow, warm water. Those illustrated are among the largest and showiest species. Most are smaller and not as attractive.

1. Bushy-backed Sea Slug

2. Plumed Sea Slug

SEA SLUGS are a paradox—shell-less shellfish. Some land snails also lack shells, however. The embryo does have a coiled shell, but this is lost soon after the Sea Slug emerges from the egg. Sea Slugs vary considerably in size and color. The Plumed Sea Slug is one of the largest American species. Most others are much smaller. These unusual animals feed partly on Sea Anemones and are able to use the stinging cells taken from their prey as part of their own body defenses. Most Sea Slugs are cold-water animals, more common in Pacific than in Atlantic waters.

SQUIDS, OCTOPUSES, and their kin are mollusks in which the foot is modified into a ring of tentacles, bearing cuplike suction discs around the mouths. Giant Octopus and Giant Squid are rare, deep-water animals. None is as big as the stories told about them. Other species of both animals are common, harmless, and often prized as food.

Squids, common along both our coasts, usually travel in schools. Most species are 8 to 20 in. long, though the Giant Squid measures up to 50 ft. The Squid's shell is reduced to a soft internal plate, the "pen." A muscular mantle covers the body. Squids are jet-propelled: they eject a stream of water that shoots them backward. Squids encircle small fish with their tentacles and eat with sharp horny beaks set around their mouths. They protect themselves by emitting an inky fluid, and hide from their enemies in this smoke screen.

Atlantic Octopus

Octopuses prefer shallower water than do Squids and are often found under rocks at low tide. They feed mostly on crabs. Both the Squids and Octopuses can change color rapidly, especially when excited or feeding. The colors are usually browns, yellows, and a dull rose. Octopuses move along the bottom using their tentacles as legs, or they swim by jet propulsion like Squids. From eggs laid in jellied clusters on rocks, the young emerge as miniature adults. Atlantic and Pacific shore species are similar in appearance.

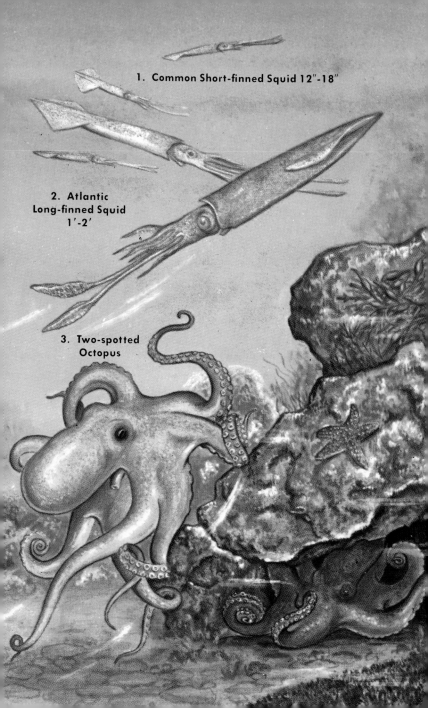

1. Common Short-finned Squid 12"-18"

2. Atlantic
Long-finned Squid
1'-2'

3. Two-spotted
Octopus

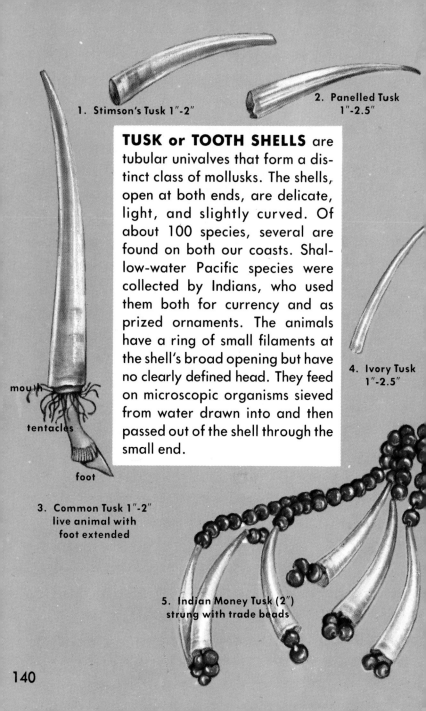

1. Stimson's Tusk 1"-2"

2. Panelled Tusk 1"-2.5"

TUSK or TOOTH SHELLS are tubular univalves that form a distinct class of mollusks. The shells, open at both ends, are delicate, light, and slightly curved. Of about 100 species, several are found on both our coasts. Shallow-water Pacific species were collected by Indians, who used them both for currency and as prized ornaments. The animals have a ring of small filaments at the shell's broad opening but have no clearly defined head. They feed on microscopic organisms sieved from water drawn into and then passed out of the shell through the small end.

4. Ivory Tusk 1"-2.5"

mouth

tentacles

foot

3. Common Tusk 1"-2" live animal with foot extended

5. Indian Money Tusk (2") strung with trade beads

Beach Plums spot dunes from Massachusetts to Virginia.

PLANTS OF DUNE AND SHORE

In the long run, all animal life of the sea depends upon primary food producers—the photosynthetic algae and plants. Seed-producing aquatic species also grow in brackish or salt water. Less important but of special interest are many land plants that have adapted to the seashore environment. Some grow on beach sands or dunes or in crevices of sea cliffs. Shore plants have deep, penetrating roots and often small leathery, hairy, or waxy leaves. A number are succulents capable of storing water and thus diluting harmful salts. All are resistant to wind and salt spray.

Of the plants along the shore, members of the grass and sedge families have been most successful. These are often less conspicuous and more difficult to identify. Other flowering plants range from small herbaceous species to shrubs and trees. The latter include, besides those illustrated, pines, cedar, hollies, sumac, and others. The herbaceous plants are more numerous and so diverse that only a few are shown on the following pages.

FLOWERS, Zim and Martin, Golden Press, New York, 1987, 1950.
TREES, Zim and Martin, Golden Press, New York, 1987, 1952.
TREES OF NORTH AMERICA, Brockman, Golden Press, New York, 1986, 1968.

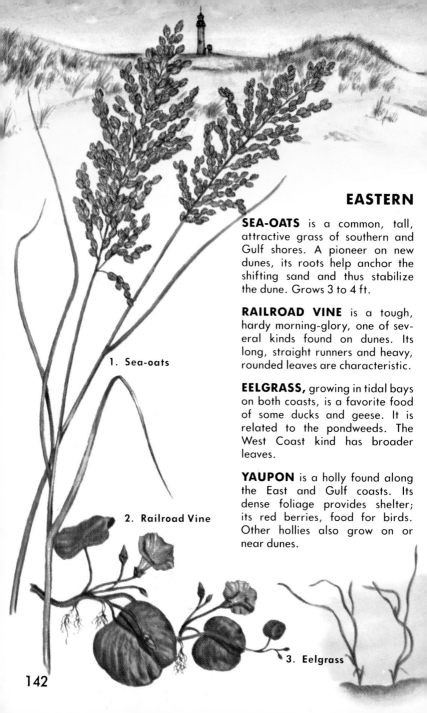

EASTERN

SEA-OATS is a common, tall, attractive grass of southern and Gulf shores. A pioneer on new dunes, its roots help anchor the shifting sand and thus stabilize the dune. Grows 3 to 4 ft.

RAILROAD VINE is a tough, hardy morning-glory, one of several kinds found on dunes. Its long, straight runners and heavy, rounded leaves are characteristic.

EELGRASS, growing in tidal bays on both coasts, is a favorite food of some ducks and geese. It is related to the pondweeds. The West Coast kind has broader leaves.

YAUPON is a holly found along the East and Gulf coasts. Its dense foliage provides shelter; its red berries, food for birds. Other hollies also grow on or near dunes.

1. Sea-oats

2. Railroad Vine

3. Eelgrass

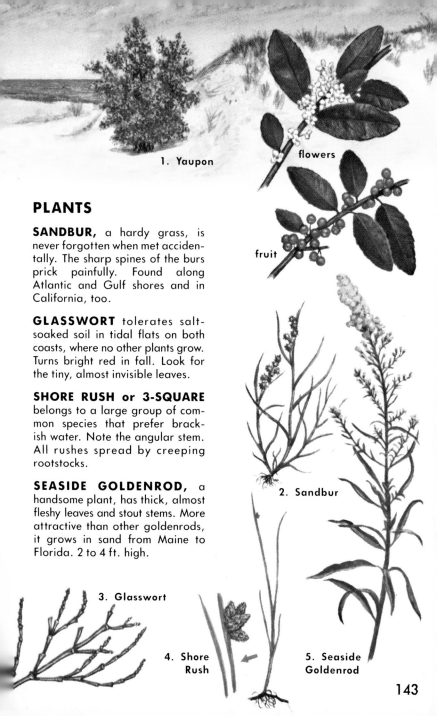

1. Yaupon

flowers

fruit

PLANTS

SANDBUR, a hardy grass, is never forgotten when met accidentally. The sharp spines of the burs prick painfully. Found along Atlantic and Gulf shores and in California, too.

GLASSWORT tolerates salt-soaked soil in tidal flats on both coasts, where no other plants grow. Turns bright red in fall. Look for the tiny, almost invisible leaves.

SHORE RUSH or 3-SQUARE belongs to a large group of common species that prefer brackish water. Note the angular stem. All rushes spread by creeping rootstocks.

SEASIDE GOLDENROD, a handsome plant, has thick, almost fleshy leaves and stout stems. More attractive than other goldenrods, it grows in sand from Maine to Florida. 2 to 4 ft. high.

2. Sandbur

3. Glasswort

4. Shore Rush

5. Seaside Goldenrod

143

WESTERN

LUPINES vary from small herbs to large shrubs. Several kinds, with spikes of attractive blue or yellow flowers, grow abundantly along western beaches. Tree Lupine is the largest of these species.

SEA-FIG and related ice plants are unusual, thick-leaved plants found along shores in many warmer countries. Sea-fig is prolific, thrifty, and attractive. Its fruit is edible.

BEACH PEAS include several species. Some are hairy; some smooth and thin-leaved. The flowers are usually purple and the seeds are in a thin pod. Beach Peas are related to sweet and garden peas.

SAND STRAWBERRY is a small, short-stemmed plant that grows on or near the beaches and also on open prairies. Blooms and fruits early in spring. The fruits are small but delicious.

1. Lupine

2. Sea-fig

3. Beach Pea

4. Sand Strawberry

5. Beach Morning-glory

PLANTS

BEACH MORNING-GLORY is one of a family that includes the common bindweed. This species, with small, purplish flowers and thick leaves, grows on sandy beaches.

REED grows commonly in mildly brackish marshes of both coasts, spreading by a fast-growing rootstock. Height: 10 ft. or more. One of the largest native grasses.

SEASIDE DAISY is a short (6 to 10 in.) plant of bluffs and beaches, with thick, hairy stems and leaves. Showy flowers bloom from April to July. Not a true daisy but a fleabane.

SAND VERBENA, in several forms, grows in the West—in deserts and along shores. All have sticky stems; small, rounded leaves; and either pink, yellow, or white flowers.

1. Reed

2. Seaside Daisy

3. Sand Verbena

a

b

145

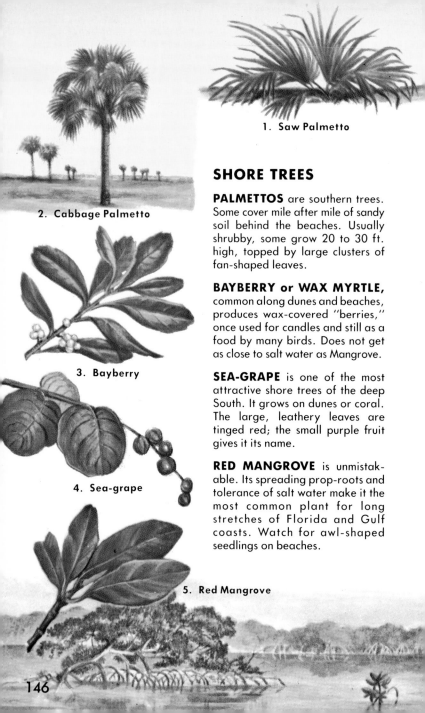

1. Saw Palmetto

2. Cabbage Palmetto

3. Bayberry

4. Sea-grape

5. Red Mangrove

SHORE TREES

PALMETTOS are southern trees. Some cover mile after mile of sandy soil behind the beaches. Usually shrubby, some grow 20 to 30 ft. high, topped by large clusters of fan-shaped leaves.

BAYBERRY or WAX MYRTLE, common along dunes and beaches, produces wax-covered "berries," once used for candles and still as a food by many birds. Does not get as close to salt water as Mangrove.

SEA-GRAPE is one of the most attractive shore trees of the deep South. It grows on dunes or coral. The large, leathery leaves are tinged red; the small purple fruit gives it its name.

RED MANGROVE is unmistakable. Its spreading prop-roots and tolerance of salt water make it the most common plant for long stretches of Florida and Gulf coasts. Watch for awl-shaped seedlings on beaches.

Brown Pelican

BIRDS of sea and shore add a sparkle of life whenever they appear. Some venture far out to sea. Others live and move along the shore, one of the best places to study birds while they are migrating. The birds in this book supplement those in BIRDS, a Golden Guide.

Birds of the shore include sandpipers, terns, pelicans, herons, gulls, ducks, and others adapted to life on water or along the shore. Many land birds live along the shores also. Seaside and Sharptailed sparrows, Boat-tailed Grackles, Tree Swallows, and larks are found in or near salt marshes. Ospreys, Bald Eagles, Crows, and Fish Crows prefer open headlands or protected bays and lagoons. In spring and fall, many migrating birds follow the shoreline. Nearly all shore birds migrate. Do more than identify birds; watch them feed and fly. See a whole flock maneuver together with unerring accuracy. Illustrations show adult birds in spring plumage. Further reading:

BIRDS, Zim and Gabrielson, Golden Press, New York, 1987, 1955.
A FIELD GUIDE TO EASTERN BIRDS and A FIELD GUIDE TO WESTERN BIRDS, Peterson, Houghton Mifflin Co., Boston, 1980, 1961.
BIRDS OF NORTH AMERICA, Robbins, Bruun, and Zim, Golden Press, New York, 1983, 1966.

OYSTERCATCHERS are waders of rocky shores of both coasts. These stocky birds, 16 to 18 in., with black heads and heavy red bills are quickly recognized. In flight the eastern species shows white wing patches. The western Black Oystercatcher has no white.

SEMIPALMATED PLOVER, a rather small (6 to 8 in.) bird with a black collar and a short bill. Often it is seen running along the sand or flying low over surf. Note its short tail and dark brown back.

RUDDY TURNSTONE (8 to 9½ in.) migrates down both coasts along sandy and rocky shores. Look for the white head and rusty brown back. In flight note the striking brown-and-white rump, tail, and wing pattern.

DOWITCHER is a snipelike bird (10½ to 12 in.) with a long, straight bill. On mud flats, sandy beaches, and salt marshes it continually probes the mud for food. Note its rusty color, whitish back and rump.

WILLETS are large (14 to 17 in.), fairly drab birds with long, straight bills and long, dark legs. Seen along both coasts, in marshes and mud flats. Identified in flight by their black-and-white wing pattern.

AVOCETS (17 to 20 in.) are marked by their long, thin, up-turned bills, and by their longer, thin black legs. Note the pale brown head and neck, and the strongly marked black-and-white wings. More common on the West Coast in quiet lagoons and on mud flats.

KNOTS are cinnamon-brown in spring; gray and white in winter. They are smaller (10 to 11 in.) than Dowitchers and have shorter bills. Common during spring and fall migrations.

SANDERLING (7 to 8 in.), common in winter on both coasts, is a stocky sandpiper showing a broad white stripe on the wings. Feeds on small invertebrates along surf or on mud flats.

PECTORAL SANDPIPERS migrate along both coasts and are partial to coastal swamps. Note the white throat and abdomen, crossed by a broad, streaked band. Legs thin and yellow; length: 8½ to 9½ in.

SEMIPALMATED SANDPIPER and the almost identical Western Sandpiper of the Pacific are very common during migrations. Streaked dark brown above with dark legs and short, dark bill. Length: 5½ to 6½ in.

149

1. Herring Gull   2. Laughing Gull

GULLS are common on all shores and along many lakes and rivers. Most common in the East is the Herring Gull (22 to 26 in.), marked by black wing tips and pinkish legs. Several other gulls are similar. The California Gull of the West Coast (20 to 23 in.) is slightly smaller, with dark legs and with a red spot near the tip of its lower bill. The Ring-billed Gull also is similar but smaller (18 to 19 in.), with a black ring around its yellowish bill and with dull yellow legs. The Western Gull is like the California Gull, but has a yellow bill with a red spot, and flesh-colored legs. The Laughing Gull is 15 to 17 in. It is black-headed in spring, and with very dark wings and back. The Great Black-backed Gull is a northern bird seen mainly in winter along Atlantic shores. Its large size (28 to 31 in.) and dark back identify it. On the East Coast the tern-related Black Skimmer is a striking bird with black back and wings, and white below. It uses its red underslung bill to scoop up small fish from close to the surface.

3. Ring-billed Gull   4. Western Gull   5. California Gull

150

1. Royal Tern 2. Common Tern

TERNS The Royal Tern is a handsome bird of southern shores—Atlantic and Pacific. Note its black, crested crown, the orange bill, and the deeply forked tail. Length: 19 to 21 in. The Caspian Tern is similar in range, size, and general appearance. It has a red bill, and tail is less forked. The Common Tern is easy to see and identify. Note its black cap, forked tail, and black-tipped orange bill. Length: 13 to 16 in. Forster's Tern, more common in the West, generally lighter, prefers marshes to open sandy beaches. The Arctic Tern is grayer, with bill completely red.

3. Arctic Tern 4. Forster's Tern 6. Great Black-backed Gull

5. Black Skimmer

WOOD STORK 34 to 38 in. Large flocks along southern shores. Note black on wings, gray head. Flies with neck out.

WHITE IBIS Smaller (22 to 26 in.), almost all white. Red face. Seen in large flocks over coastal swamps.

DOUBLE-CRESTED CORMO-RANT ranges farther north than others on this page. Often suns with wings half open, drying them. Large (28 to 34 in.).

WATER TURKEY or ANHINGA Prefers marshes, lagoons, coastal rivers. Glossy, greenish-gray back, with light wing patches.

GREAT BLUE HERON 40 to 50 in. Common both coasts. Great White Heron of Florida is larger, pure white, yellow bill and legs.

LITTLE BLUE HERON 20 to 25 in. Young: white or blue-blotched. Green Heron smaller; yellow legs, white on throat. Both coasts.

REDDISH EGRET 28 to 32 in.; on warmer coasts of both oceans. A white phase is similar to Common Egret.

GREAT EGRET 34 to 40 in. Common on both coasts. Snowy Egret is 8 to 24 in., has yellow feet, black bill and legs.

BOOKS FOR FURTHER STUDY   Systematic and exact identification is often difficult. You may need the aid of technical publications, such as journals of scientific societies and museums. Less technical books include:

Abbott, R. Tucker, AMERICAN SEASHELLS, Van Nostrand Reinhold, 1974.

Abbott, R. Tucker, SEASHELLS OF NORTH AMERICA, Golden Press, 1986, 1968.

Carson, Rachel, THE EDGE OF THE SEA, New American Library, 1955.

Costello, David, THE SEASHORE WORLD, Crowell, 1980.

Gosner, Kenneth, A FIELD GUIDE TO THE ATLANTIC SEASHORE, Houghton Mifflin, 1979.

Meinkoth, Norman, FIELD GUIDE TO NORTH AMERICAN SEASHORE CREATURES, Alfred A. Knopf, 1981.

Riccuiti, Edward R., THE BEACHWALKER'S GUIDE, Doubleday, 1982.

Sackett, Russell, EDGE OF THE SEA, Time-Life Books, 1983.

Voss, Gilbert L., SEASHORE LIFE OF FLORIDA AND THE CARIBBEAN, E. A. Seamann, 1976.

MUSEUMS, AQUARIA, AND MARINE BIOLOGICAL STATIONS

American Museum of Natural History, New York, N.Y.

Chicago Museum of Natural History, Chicago, Ill.

Shedd Aquarium, Chicago, Ill.

Rosenstiel School of Marine and Atmospheric Science, Univ. of Miami, Miami, Fla.

Oceanographic Institute of Florida State Univ., Alligator Harbor, Fla.

Gulf Coast Research Laboratory, Ocean Springs, Miss.

Hopkins Marine Station, Pacific Grove, Calif.

Puget Sound Marine Biol. Station, Univ. of Wash., Friday Harbor, Wash.

Scripps Institution of Oceanography, Univ. of Calif., La Jolla, Calif.

National Marine Fisheries Service Center Aquarium, Woods Hole, Mass.

North Carolina Marine Resources Center, Boque Bank, N.C.

Hampton Mariner's Museum, Beaufort, N.C.

SCIENTIFIC NAMES

Following are the scientific names of species illustrated in this book. Heavy type indicates pages where species appear; numbers in lighter type are caption numbers. The genus name is first, then the species. If the genus name is abbreviated, it is the same as the genus name mentioned just before it.

3 Mnemiopsis leidyi.
20 Microcoleus lyngbyaceus.
21 Codium fragile.
22 1. Cladophora sericea; 2. Ulva lactuca; 3a. Enteromorpha intestinalis; 3b. E. compressa.
23 1. Caulerpa prolifera; 2. Bryopsis plumosa.

24 1. Halimeda tuna; 2. Acetabularia crenulata; 3. Penicillus dumetosus.
25 1a. Sargassum natans; 1b. S. filipendula.
26 1. Alaria esculenta; 2. Padina pavonia; 3. Chordaria flagelliformis.
27 1. Ectocarpus viridis; 2a. Des-

marestia viridis; 2b. D. aculeata; 3. Chorda tomentosa.

28 1. Agarum cribrosum; 2a. Laminaria saccharina; 2b. L. digitata.

29 1. Macrocystis pyrifera; 2. Postelsia palmaeformis; 3. Nereocystis luetkeana.

30 1a. Fucus vesiculosus; 1b. F. distichus evanescens.

31 Dasya sp.

32 1a. Gigartina stellata; 1b. G. corymbifera; 1c. G. microphylla; 2. Chondrus crispus (3 forms); 3a. Gelidium coulteri; 3b. G. sesquipedale.

33 1a. Polysiphonia fibrillosa; 1b. P. nigrescens; 1c. P. harveyi; 2. Grinnellia americana; 3a. Spermothamnion repens; 3b. Callithamnion baileyi.

34 1a. Ceramium fastigiatum; 1b. C. rubrum; 2a. Plumaria elegans; 2b. Ptilota serrata; 3a. Porphyra umbilicalis; 3b. P. leucosticta.

35 Corallina officinalis.

40 1. Ciona intestinalis; 2. Molgula manhattensis.

41 1. Leucosolenia botryoides; 2. Scypha sp.

42 1. Microciona prolifera; 2. Cliona celata.

43 1. Callyspongia vaginalis; 2. Haliclona oculata; 3. Hippiospongia lachne; 4. H. canaliculata; 5. H. equinoformis.

45 1. Aurelia aurita; 2. Cyanea capillata.

46 1. Gonionemus vertens; 2. Tubularia spectabilis; 3. Obelia sp.

47 Physalia physalis.

48 1. Metridium senile; 2. Calliactis tricolor; 3a. Sagartia modesta; 3b. Haliplanella luciae.

49 Anthopleura xanthogrammica.

50 1. Balanophylla elegans; 2. Astrangia danae; 3. Oculina diffusa.

51 1. Corallium rubrum; 2. Agaricia agaricites; 3. Acropora cervicornis; 4. Favia fragrum; 5. Diploria labyrinthiformis.

52 1. Pennatula aculeata; 2. Gorgonia flabellum; 3. Plexaura flexuosa.

53 1. Folia parallela; 2. Pleurobrachia brunnea.

54 Cerebratulus lacteus.

55 Nereis virens.

56 Bispira sp.

57 1. Aphrodite aculeata; 2. Pectinaria gouldii; 3. Cirratulus grandis; 4. Chaetopterus variopedatus; 5. Arenicola cristata.

58 1. Membranipora pilosa; 2. Bugula turrita; 3. Crisea eburnea.

59 1. Terebratulina spitzbergensis; 2. T. septentrionalis; 3. Lingula anatina.

61 1. Amphipholis squamata; 2. Gorgonocephalus arcticus; 3. Ophioderma brevispina; 4. Ophiopholis aculeata; 5. Ophiothrix angulata.

62 1. Henricia sanguinolenta; 2. Ctenodiscus crispatus; 3. Asterias vulgaris; 4. Solaster endeca; 5. Echinaster sentus; 6. Asterias forbesi.

63 1. Patiria miniata; 2. Linckia columbiae; 3. Henricia leviuscula; 4. Pycnopodia helianthoides; 5. Pisaster ochraceus.

64 1. Cidaris tribuloides; 2. Arbacia punctulata; 3. Echinarachnius parma.

65 1. Arbacia punctulata; 2. Strongylocentrotus droebachiensis; 3. S. franciscanus; 4. Echinometra lucunter; 5. Encope emarginata; 6. Dendraster excentricus; 7. Echinarachinus parma.

66 1. Stichopus californicus; 2. Leptosynapta tenuis; 3. Caudina arenata; 4. Cucumaria frondosa.

68 1. Lepas fascicularis; 2. Balanus balanoides.

69 1. Gammarus locusta; 2. Talorchestia longicornis; 3. Orchestoidea californiana; 4. Orchestia agilis.

70 1. Squilla empusa; 2. Penaeus setiferus; 3. Crangon septemspinosa.

71 1. Homarus americanus; 2. Panulirus argus.

72 1. Emerita analoga; 2. E. talpoida.

73 Pagurus pollicaris.

74 1. Callinectes sapidus; 2. Carcinus maenas.

75 1. Portunus gibbesii; 2. Ovalipes ocellatus.

76 1. Cancer irroratus; 2. C. borealis; 3. C. magister.

(Scientific Names Continued)

77 1. Uca pugnax; 2. Ocypode quadrata.

78 1. Pugettia producta; 2. Libinia emarginata; 3. L. dubia.

79 1. Eurypterus fischeri; 2. Limulus polyphemus.

81 1. Chaetopleura apiculata; 2. Mopalia ciliata; 3. Ischnochiton magdalensis.

83 1. Nucula proxima; 2. Acila castrensis; 3. Nuculana minuta; 4. N. taphria; 5. N. acuta.

84 1. Arca imbricata; 2. Anadara ovalis; 3. Arca zebra; 4. Anadara notabilis; 5. Barbatia bailyi.

85 1. Mytilus edulis; 2. Geukensia demissa; 3. Modiolus modiolus; 4. Ischadium recurvum.

86 1. Argopecten gibbus; 2. Chlamys ornatus; 3. Hinnites giganteus.

87 1. Pecten hericius; 2. Leptopecten latiauratus; 3. Chlamys sentis; 4. Placopecten magellanicus; 5. Pecten diegensis; 6. Argopecten irradians.

88 1. Anomia simplex; 2. A. squamula; 3. A. peruviana.

89 1. Ostrea lurida; 2. Crassostrea virginica.

90 1. Atrina serrata; 2. A. rigida; 3. Pinna carnea.

91 1. Pteria colymbus; 2. Pinctada imbricata.

92 1. Pandora gouldiana; 2. P. trilineata; 3. P. punctata; 4. P. filosa.

93 1. Astarte undata; 2. A. castanea; 3. A. borealis; 4. A. alaskensis; 5. A. esquimalti.

94 1. Pseudomiltha floridana; 2. Phacoides annulatus; 3. Codakia orbicularis; 4. Linga pensylvanica.

95 1. Clinocardium ciliatum; 2. Trachycardium muricatum; 3. Clinocardium nuttalli; 4. Dinocardium robustum.

96 1. Mercenaria campechiensis; 2. M. mercenaria.

98 1. Protothaca tenerrima; 2. P. staminea; 3. P. staminea var. laciniata.

99 1. Macrocallista maculata; 2. M. nimbosa.

100 1. Dosinia elegans; 2. D. discus; 3. Gemma gemma.

101 Tivela stultorum.

102 1. Tellina bodegensis; 2. T. carpenteri; 3. T. radiata; 4. T. nucu-

loides; 5. T. modesta; 6. T. interrupta; 7. T. lineata.

103 1. Macoma tenta; 2. M. balthica; 3. M. constricta; 4. M. secta; 5. M. indentata; 6. M. nasuta.

104 1. Donax denticulatus; 2. D. fossor; 3. D. californicus; 4. D. gouldi; 5. D. variabilis.

105 1. Solen rosaceus; 2. Ensis directus; 3. Solen viridis; 4. Tagelus plebeius.

106 1. Mactra fragilis; 2. Spisula solidissima.

107 1. Mulinia lateralis; 2. Anatina anatina; 3. Raeta plicatella.

108 1. Mya truncata; 2. M. arenaria.

109 1. Cyrtopleura costata; 2. Petricola pholadiformis; 3. Barnea truncata.

110 Teredo navalis.

112 1. Megathura crenulata; 2. Diodora aspera; 3. Acmedea antillarum; 4. Diodora listeri; 5. Notoacmea testudinalis.

113 1. Turbo castanea; 2. Calliostoma ligatum; 3. Margarites groenlandicus; 4. Calliostoma jujubinum; 5. C. canaliculatum.

114 1. Tegula funebralis; 2. T. gallina; 3. T. fasciata.

115 1. Haliotis refuscens; 2. H. kamtschatkana; 3. H. fulgens; 4. H. cracherodi.

116 1. Epitonium rupicola; 2. Boreoscala greenlandica; 3. Opalia wroblewskii; 4. Epitonium multistriatum.

117 1. Natica clausa; 2. N. canrena; 3. Polinices duplicatus; 4. Lunatia heros.

118 1. Crepidula onyx; 2. C. aculeata; 3. C. nummaria; 4. C. fornicata; 5. C. convexa; 6. C. plana.

119 1. Littorina scutulata; 2. L. planaxis; 3. L. saxatilis; 4. L. irrorata; 5. L. littorea; 6. L. angulifera.

120 1. Strombus raninus; 2. Cassis tuberosa; 3. Strombus alatus.

121 1. Strombus pugilis; 2. S. gigas; 3. Cassis madagascariensis; 4. C. flammea.

122 1. Bittium alternatum; 2. Cerithidea californica; 3. Batillaria minima; 4. Cerithium atratum.

123 1. Tonna galea; 2. T. maculosa; 3. Ficus communis.

156

125 1. Cypraea spadicea; 2. C. spurca acicularis; 3. C. cinerea; 4. C. zebra; 5. Trivia solandri; 6. T. californiana; 7. T. quadripunctata; 8. T. pediculus.

126 1. Phyllonotus pomum; 2. Chicoreus dilectus; 3. Eupleura caudata; 4. Maxwellia gemma.

127 1. Pteropurpura festivus; 2. P. trialata; 3. Murex cabriti; 4. Ocenebra interfossa; 5. O. circumtexta.

128 1. Purpura patula; 2. Urosalpinx cinerea; 3. Nucella lima; 4. N. emarginata; 5. N. lapillus.

129 1. Nitidella carinata; 2. Mitrella lunata; 3. Columbella mercatoria; 4. Anachis avara.

130 1. Busycotypus cannaliculatus; 2. Busycon carica; 3. Neptunea tabulata; 4. N. decemcostata.

131 1. Busycon contrarium; 2. Busycotypus spiratus; 3. Buccinum undatum; 4. B. glaciale.

132 1. Ilyanassa obsoleta; 2. Nassarius vibex; 3. N. trivittatus; 4. N. fossatus.

133 1. Fasciolaria hunteria; 2. Pleuroploca gigantea; 3. Fasciolaria tulipa.

134 1. Oliva sayana; 2. Olivella mutica; 3. O. baetica; 4. O. biplicata.

135 1. Conus californicus; 2. C. mus; 3. C. regius; 4. C. floridanus; 5. C. spurius.

136 1. Bulla gouldiana; 2. Haminoea solitaria; 3. Hydatina vesicaria; 4. Bulla occidentalis; 5. B. striata.

137 1. Dendronotus frondosus; 2. Aeolis papillosa.

138 Octopus vulgaris.

139 1. Illex illecebrosus; 2. Loligo pealei; 3. Octopus bimaculatus.

140 1. Antalis entale stimsoni; 2. Dentalium laqueatum; 3. D. entale; 4. Graptaeme eboreum; 5. D. pretiosum.

141 Prunus maritimus.

142 1. Uniola paniculata; 2. Impomoea pes-caprae; 3. Zostera marina.

143 1. Ilex vomitoria; 2. Cenchrus tribuloides; 3. Salicornia europaea; 4. Scirpus americanus; 5. Solidago sempervirens.

144 1. Lupinus arboreus; 2. Mesembryanthemum chilense; 3. Lathyrus japonicus; 4. Fragaria chiloensis; 5. Convolvulus soldanella.

145 1. Phragmites communis; 2. Erigeron glaucus; 3a. Abronia umbellata; 3b. A. latifolia.

146 1. Serenoa repens; 2. Sabal palmetto; 3. Myrica cerifera; 4. Coccoloba uvifera; 5. Rhizophora mangle.

147 Pelacanus occidentalis.

148 1. Haematopus palliatus; 2. Charadrius semipalmatus; 3. Arenaria interpres; 4. Limnodromus griseus; 5. Catoptrophorus semipalmatus.

149 1. Recurvirostra americana; 2. Calidris canutus; 3. C. alba; 4. C. melanotos; 5. C. mauri.

150 1. Larus argentatus; 2. L. atricilla; 3. L. delawarensis; 4. L. occidentalis; 5. L. californicus.

151 1. Sterna maxima; 2. S. hirundo; 3. S. paradisaea; 4. S. forsteri; 5. Rynchops niger; 6. Larus marinus.

152 1. Mycteria americana; 2. Eudocimus albus; 3. Phalacrocorax auritus; 4. Anhinga anhinga.

153 1. Ardea herodias; 2. Egretta caerulea; 3. Dichromanassa rufescens; 4. Casmerodius albus.

Measuring scale (in millimeters and centimeters)

MEASURING SCALE (IN 10THS OF AN INCH)